# LEO
# TOLSTOY

COMPREHENSIVE RESEARCH
AND STUDY GUIDE

## BLOOM'S
## MAJOR
## NOVELISTS

EDITED AND WITH AN
INTRODUCTION BY HAROLD BLOOM

## BLOOM'S MAJOR DRAMATISTS

Aeschylus

Anton Chekhov

Aristophanes

Berthold Brecht

Euripides

Henrik Ibsen

Ben Jonson

Christopher Marlowe

Arthur Miller

Eugene O'Neill

Shakespeare's Comedies

Shakespeare's Histories

Shakespeare's Romances

Shakespeare's Tragedies

George Bernard Shaw

Neil Simon

Sophocles

Oscar Wilde

Tennessee Williams

August Wilson

## BLOOM'S MAJOR NOVELISTS

Jane Austen

The Brontës

Willa Cather

Stephen Crane

Charles Dickens

Fyodor Dostoevsky

William Faulkner

F. Scott Fitzgerald

Thomas Hardy

Nathaniel Hawthorne

Ernest Hemingway

Henry James

James Joyce

D. H. Lawrence

Toni Morrison

John Steinbeck

Stendhal

Leo Tolstoy

Mark Twain

Alice Walker

Edith Wharton

Virginia Woolf

## BLOOM'S MAJOR WORLD POETS

Geoffrey Chaucer

Emily Dickinson

John Donne

T. S. Eliot

Robert Frost

Langston Hughes

John Milton

Edgar Allan Poe

Poets of World War I

Shakespeare's Poems & Sonnets

Alfred, Lord Tennyson

Walt Whitman

William Wordsworth

## BLOOM'S MAJOR SHORT STORY WRITERS

William Faulkner

F. Scott Fitzgerald

Ernest Hemingway

O. Henry

James Joyce

Herman Melville

Flannery O'Connor

Edgar Allan Poe

J. D. Salinger

John Steinbeck

Mark Twain

Eudora Welty

# LEO
# TOLSTOY

COMPREHENSIVE RESEARCH
AND STUDY GUIDE

## BLOOM'S
MAJOR
## NOVELISTS

EDITED AND WITH AN INTRODUCTION
BY HAROLD BLOOM

Printed and bound in the United States of America.

First Printing
1 3 5 7 9 8 6 4 2

Library of Congress Cataloging-in-Publication Data
Leo Tolstoy / edited and with an introduction by Harold Bloom.
        p. cm. —(Bloom's major novelists)
    Includes bibliographical references and index.
    ISBN 0-7910-6347-X (alk. paper)
        1. Tolstoy, Leo, graf, 1828–1910—Examinations—Study guides.
    2. Tolstoy, Leo, graf, 1828–1910—Criticism and interpretation.
    I. Bloom, Harold. II. Series.

PG3410 .L415 2001
891.73'3—dc21                          2001053678


Chelsea House Publishers
1974 Sproul Road, Suite 400
Broomall, PA 19008-0914

The Chelsea House World Wide Web address is
http://www.chelseahouse.com

Series Editor: Matt Uhler

Contributing Editor: Portia Williams Weiskel

Produced by Publisher's Services, Santa Barbara, California

# Contents

# User's Guide

This volume is designed to present biographical, critical, and bibliographical information on the author's best-known or most important works. Following Harold Bloom's editor's note and introduction is a detailed biography of the author, discussing major life events and important literary accomplishments. A plot summary of each novel follows, tracing significant themes, patterns, and motifs in the work.

A selection of critical extracts, derived from previously published material from leading critics, analyzes aspects of each work. The extracts consist of statements from the author, if available, early reviews of the work, and later evaluations up to the present. A bibliography of the author's writings (including a complete list of all works written, cowritten, edited, and translated), a list of additional books and articles on the author and his or her work, and an index of themes and ideas in the author's writings conclude the volume.

**Harold Bloom** is Sterling Professor of the Humanities at Yale University and Henry W. and Albert A. Berg Professor of English at the New York University Graduate School. He is the author of over 20 books, including *Shelley's Mythmaking* (1959), *The Visionary Company* (1961), *Blake's Apocalypse* (1963), *Yeats* (1970), *A Map of Misreading* (1975), *Kabbalah and Criticism* (1975), *Agon: Toward a Theory of Revisionism* (1982), *The American Religion* (1992), *The Western Canon* (1994), and *Omens of Millennium: The Gnosis of Angels, Dreams, and Resurrection* (1996). *The Anxiety of Influence* (1973) sets forth Professor Bloom's provocative theory of the literary relationships between the great writers and their predecessors. His most recent books include *Shakespeare: The Invention of the Human,* a 1998 National Book Award finalist, and *How to Read and Why,* which was published in 2000.

Professor Bloom earned his Ph.D. from Yale University in 1955 and has served on the Yale faculty since then. He is a 1985 MacArthur Foundation Award recipient, served as the Charles Eliot Norton Professor of Poetry at Harvard University in 1987–88, and has received honorary degrees from the universities of Rome and Bologna. In 1999, Professor Bloom received the prestigious American Academy of Arts and Letters Gold Medal for Criticism.

Currently, Harold Bloom is the editor of numerous Chelsea House volumes of literary criticism, including the series BLOOM'S NOTES, BLOOM'S MAJOR DRAMATISTS, BLOOM'S MAJOR NOVELISTS, MAJOR LITERARY CHARACTERS, MODERN CRITICAL VIEWS, MODERN CRITICAL INTERPRETATIONS, and WOMEN WRITERS OF ENGLISH AND THEIR WORKS.

# Editor's Note

My Introduction meditates upon *War and Peace,* and contrasts Tolstoy's Homeric aspiration to his involuntary Shakespeareanism.

Critical views on *War and Peace* commence with the novelist Turgenev, who progresses from irritation with the epic novel to a sense that Tolstoy touches the earth and rises up in strength. An anonymous British reviewer of 1886 finds in the book "the unrest of life itself," while Tolstoy's friendly critic, Strakhov, celebrates the mastery of realism. Lenin criticizes Tolstoy for anti-revolutionary attitudes, after which Percy Lubbock wrongly finds *War and Peace* to be formless.

Virginia Woolf exalts Tolstoy as the greatest of all novelists, while G. K. Chesterton finds in the Russian visionary the virtue of vitalistic simplification. For James T. Farrell, Tolstoy's greatness is in his moral originality, after which Isaiah Berlin catches the paradox of Tolstoy's great insight: we are not free, but cannot live without the sense that freedom is possible for us.

Albert Cook praises Tolstoy's power of portraying moral character, while both R. F. Christian and Ernest J. Simmons also investigate Tolstoy's art of characterization. The novelist's attachment both to the *Iliad* and the Gospels is charted by E. B. Greenwood, after which A. V. Knowles judges early Russian criticism of *War and Peace* to have been plainly inadequate to the book's sublimity.

The Wordsworthian element in Tolstoy is expounded by Henry Gifford, while Gary Saul Morson emphasizes *War and Peace*'s control of perspective. Tolstoy's variety of anti-Westernism is investigated by Rimvydas Silbajoris, after which Natasha Sankovitch examines the force of deliberate repetition in Tolstoy's vision of reality.

Critical views on *Anna Karenina* begin with Dostoevsky, who in his *Diary of a Writer* praises Tolstoy for manifesting a Russian view of evil, rather than a Western one. A Western anonymous reviewer follows with a similar view of Anna's sin and its consequences, and the English critic Matthew Arnold seems to agree, though he finds Anna charming.

The biographer Derrick Leon explores links between Levin and Tolstoy, while James T. Farrell sees Tolstoy rejecting the American Way. R. P. Blackmur commends Anna and Levin for their apprehensions of immediate experience, after which Lionel Trilling notes that: "for Tolstoy everyone and everything has saving grace."

Renato Poggioli analyzes Tolstoy's motives for not portraying the consummation of Anna's love for Vronsky, while Ernest J. Simmons defends Anna's passion as "irresistible." Elizabeth Gunn's formula for this is: "we are to blame but we are not to blame."

Elisabeth Stenbock-Fermor links Tolstoy's exaltation of the family to his similar sense that tilling the Russian soil was sacred. Tragedy is invoked by E. B. Greenwood as the category that keeps Anna's fate from being mere mortal punishment.

Why does Anna kill herself? Edward Wasiolek suggests that it is because she comes to realize that she embodies the wrong kind of love: coercive and alienating. But for Malcolm Jones, failure in communication with Vronsky dooms Anna, while Joan Delaney Grossman sees the lovers' poor communication as a mutual failure of character.

Natasha Sankovitch finds a defect in forgiveness within Anna herself, after which James Wood shrewdly observes that Tolstoy's characters, like Shakespeare's, are real to us because they are so real to themselves.

# Introduction

## HAROLD BLOOM

Cervantes, the first novelist, and Proust and Joyce, the final ones, have in common with Tolstoy that they all transcend the form of the novel. *Don Quixote* is the metaphysical comedy of the Spanish psyche, even as Proust and Joyce divide the twentieth-century Western psyche between them. All three—Cervantes, Proust, Joyce— have epic scope and drive. In the midst of the novel's tradition, the culminating master was Tolstoy, rather than Goethe, Dickens, Balzac, or Manzoni, let alone Henry James, who rather desperately preferred Turgenev to Tolstoy. James peculiarly compared *War and Peace* to *The Three Musketeers,* describing both as "large loose baggy monsters." Though Henry James is admired for his criticism, I find him remarkably inconsistent. He is misleading and wrong on Hawthorne and Whitman, George Eliot and Dickens, and on Tolstoy he is plainly out of court.

Tolstoy—like the Bible, Homer, and Shakespeare—defeats criticism. He associated himself with the Bible and Homer, and denounced Shakespeare, but owed much to his reviled precursor. To be a larger, more universal writer than Tolstoy is improbable, unless you are Shakespeare. I join John Bayley in noting that Tolstoy accepts only one character in Shakespeare: Falstaff. Falstaff, among all Shakespearean characters—according to Tolstoy—is unique in not acting the part of himself: "He alone speaks in a way proper to himself." Falstaff, like Tolstoy's protagonists, participates in the common life. So of course do hundreds of others in Shakespeare, yet it fascinates me that Falstaff overcomes Tolstoy's moral objections to Shakespeare.

Tolstoy demands that art be accessible to everyone. Since Shakespeare more even than Tolstoy and Dickens has that universal appeal, Tolstoy had to defend himself. If we turn inside out Tolstoy's rejection of Shakespeare, then we have an entry into Tolstoy's own greatness, as the other poet of human nature. In Tolstoy (as in Shakespeare), the art itself is nature. Shakespeare, notoriously indifferent to plots, would take his from anywhere: the sense of ongoing life, in Shakespeare and in Tolstoy, subsumes any plot whatsoever.

Tolstoy, without vainglory, associated himself with Homer. The juxtaposition with the *Iliad* would destroy almost any other narrative work, but not *War and Peace*. And yet Tolstoy truly resembles Shakespeare and not Homer, angry as he would have been to hear such a judgment. Dostoevsky loved Shakespeare and drew on him freely; Tolstoy despised Shakespeare, and drew on him involuntarily. After Shakespeare, the inwardness of literary character is Shakespearean, or simply does not exist. Goethe came to understand this, as did Turgenev, Dostoevsky, Stendhal, Victor Hugo, Emerson and a myriad of others, but Tolstoy was furious at Shakespeare's pragmatic freedom from Christianity. I am not at all clear as to just what even Tolstoy's rationalized Christianity has to do with *War and Peace,* or with *Anna Karenina*. What matters most in Tolstoy is his altogether Shakespearean gift for individualizing even his minor characters. Shakespeare remains, after four centuries, the greatest of all psychologists, and where else but in Shakespeare could Tolstoy learn his own depth as a psychologist? It is weirdly appropriate that the first sketches of *War and Peace* were entitled *All's Well that Ends Well*. Rereading *War and Peace,* with its effective, almost theatrical alternation of scenes, I also begin to ask: where, but from Shakespeare, did Tolstoy acquire his sense of scene-shifting as a further index to the clash of personalities?

Thomas Mann got it right when he ascribed Tolstoy's hatred of Shakespeare to "antagonism against that universal and all-accepting nature: in the jealousy which a man enduring moral torment was bound to feel in face of the blithe irony of an absolutely creative genius." I wonder if Mann does not give us another clue as to why the philosopher Wittgenstein, who was so fiercely devoted to Tolstoy, was also distrustful of Shakespeare. Wittgenstein insisted that: "There are, indeed, things that cannot be put into words." Incessantly rereading Shakespeare, I doubt Wittgenstein, as there is nothing that Shakespeare cannot get into his more than twenty-one thousand words.

Viktor Shklovsky famously called attention to Tolstoy's art of "making it strange," of "refusing to recognize an object, of describing it as if it were seen for the first time." Tolstoy sought and achieved originality in object-representation, but his modes of portraying personality and character at their best recall Shakespeare's, an observation that would have infuriated Tolstoy. The extraordinary changes in

Pierre, in *War and Peace,* follow the Shakespearean paradigm of surprise through involuntary self-overhearing. Tolstoy, who feared his own nihilism, and who secretly had identified God with death, accurately saw that Shakespeare was free of dogmatic shadows, and that Lear's tragedy, and Macbeth's, reflected Shakespeare's pragmatic nihilism. Shakespeare was perhaps the least solipsistic of all great writers; Tolstoy, the most. Tolstoy's resentment of Shakespeare was genius recognizing its antagonist in an opposed genius.

Of all Shakespearean roles, Tolstoy most resented Lear's, as he accurately perceived that King Lear was a pagan play directed to a Christian audience. In 1910, at eighty-two, Tolstoy fled his wife and family, to die at a railway station. The image of Lear's death was not in Tolstoy's mind, but it is difficult to keep it away from ours as we contemplate Tolstoy's desperate end. ❀

# Biography of
# Leo Tolstoy

When Leo Tolstoy was five he joined the Ant Brothers, an imaginary sect associated with a sacred secret about enduring human happiness. Access to the secret (said to be carved on a green stick) and other magical pleasures could be had by performing inventive tasks such as standing in a corner without thinking of a white bear. (Tolstoy always failed.) Such formidable tasks did not prevent the four brothers from contemplating the secret's meaning. At his request, Tolstoy was buried near the stick 77 years later.

The burial site was also his place of birth—the ancestral estate Yasnaya Polyana (meaning "Clear Fields"), 100 miles south of Moscow. After early losses of both parents, the children were devotedly raised by family members, and their childhood—despite these losses—passed in the idyllic landscape of wide meadows, forests, and barnyard. At every turn were formative influences. Once, after a peasant remarked that his horse was exhausted, Tolstoy jumped off, apologized, and vowed never again to harm an animal. Later in life, Tolstoy's doctrine of nonviolence included vegetarianism. Questions of life's meaning and the importance of love—which became Tolstoy's mission to discover and articulate—permeated the inarticulate experiences of his childhood.

Tolstoy descended from old aristocracy whose bestowed blessings included a proper education. In 1836 the family reluctantly moved to Moscow where Tolstoy was tutored by a likable German and a less likeable French aesthete who gave impetus to Tolstoy's lifelong hatred of violence by locking him in a room. Beyond the influence of tutors Tolstoy had other intense experiences: the intoxication of romantic attachments and preoccupation with metaphysical questions.

A happy return to Yasnaya Polyana was cut short by deaths in the family. Tolstoy went to live in Kazan, the social capital of Russia. Entering young manhood without his beloved aunt Tatiana was the beginning of a turbulent period. He disliked the city's superficiality and his own appearance which he found so disagreeable that he restyled himself to look like Byron. He was vain, melancholy, eccentric, and painfully sensitive. After briefly entertaining a notion that he could fly he entered a period of severe skepticism believing himself to be alone in the universe. Books, music, and sustained friendships were his consolations.

Tolstoy's youth coincided with the the period of Russian history preceding the Crimean War (1853–1856). He attended Kazan University but—indignant over academic formalities—left without a degree. Back at Yasnaya Polyana he made some enlightened attempts to improve the condition of his serfs, contined to read, and lost money at card games. Like other young confessional writers (Joyce, Rousseau, St. Augustine) Tolstoy was alternately seduced and repelled by sensual pleasure. He took up the practice, inspired by Benjamin Franklin, of recording his failings in a journal with the goal of self-perfection. Early diaries reveal the incongruous personalities he was trying out. An outstanding feature of his writing is precisely this ability to encompass and articulate a range of vividly believable characters.

Tolstoy was rescued from this directionless period by brother Nikolai who persuaded him to join the army. In 1853 he defended the fortress at Sevastopol during the Crimean War where he discovered first-hand the unforgettably grim details of war. Battle scenes from *War and Peace* reflect the writer's intimate knowledge of face-to-face combat which he relentlessly deglorifies. Military service introduced him as well to the majestic Russian landscapes—instilling a religious awe that never left him. Published sketches of his combat experience brought him early fame and encounters with censorship. *Sevastopol in May* (1855) enraged the censors who slashed all mention of the unheroic and concern for injustices done to the common soldier. Defiant and loyal to the memory of the green stick, Tolstoy wrote, "The hero of my tale—whom I love with all the power of my soul . . . is . . . Truth." In 1859 Tolstoy studied educational reform in Europe and returned to found a school at Yasnaya Polyana where children and peasants were reportedly happy. The wrenchingly painful death of brother Nikolai in 1861 left Tolstoy in despair.

In 1862 Tolstoy married Sofya Behrs, a beautiful and cultured woman. Of fifteen children seven survived. Early family life was simple and mainly harmonious.

The remaining years were devoted to writing and engagement in social issues. It was said about Tolstoy that his conscience never slept. The writings of Marx and Dostoevski were defining influences in this period. The Emancipation of the Serfs (1861) had produced an urban poverty that devastated Tolstoy. Anyone doubting the power of writers to influence lives should see the 1983 film "The Year of Living Dangerously" in which Billy the compassionate foreign correspondent in Jakarta, witnessing Sukarno's broken promises to his people, repeats obsessively the title of Tolstoy's essay "What Then Must We Do?" published in 1886 in response to the sight of human misery in Moscow.

Tolstoy's concerns overlapped those of Marx but led to different solutions. Calling the Sermon on the Mount a social document, he turned to putting his own estate in order, thus rejecting the purely political focus of Marx. His notion of "bread labor"—all must labor to feed themselves with no class serving another—impressed the revolutionaries but his famous declaration of nonviolent resistance to evil infuriated them.

During this period Tolstoy produced pamphlets on famine, religious persecution, and the democratic purposes of art. In 1891, in response to the failed harvest, he opened a soup kitchen. The dying Turgenev implored Tolstoy to return to writing, but Tolstoy—still animated by the memory of the green stick—insisted that life and art serve the same high purpose.

In 1878 Tolstoy abandoned Orthodox Christianity, judging it too aligned with state interests, and was excommunicated. Like an old Testament prophet, he continued to preach a radical and nonviolent Christianity that inspired great social visionaries like Gandhi, Chekhov, Boris Pasternak, and Martin Luther King.

During the last decade of Tolstoy's life Russia was chaotic and desperate: Lenin returned from Siberia; Stalin turned revolutionary; Jews were massacred; workers mutinied. In 1908, Tolstoy wrote a bold statement condemning capital punishment ("I Cannot Be Silent"). Police seized papers from his homestead in 1907 and some followers were imprisoned.

Although Tolstoy exhibited some moral intransigence in his final years, he continued to be compassionate and insightful. Youthful indulgences had yielded to austerity and healthful living. At 70 a vigorous Tolstoy was riding his bicycle and performing beloved farm labors. His final public statements included a warning—still relevant—of human calamity ensuing from the modern trend of replacing spiritual depth with technological progress.

In the middle of the night in October 1910 Tolstoy suddenly left home. The immediate cause was estrangement from his wife (to whom he had been faithful for 47 years) over the issue of Tolstoy's plan—his own response to "What Then Shall We Do?"—to give away his property and live an ascetic life. He died a month later, 50 miles from home, in a remote railroad station. Reportedly his last words were: "To seek, always to seek. . . ." Tolstoy's departure and death were sensational events. People stood, hats off and weeping, when his death was announced. The Soviet Union declared 1910— the 50th anniversary of his death— "the Year of Tolstoy" though it remained officially ambivalent: praising his condemnation of suffering caused by private property, criticizing his failure to see the historical need for violent revolution.

As storyteller, Tolstoy is compared to Dickens; for intellectual insight, to Schopenhauer. For his social vision he worked for the Kingdom of God on earth. He continues to be regarded among the greatest writers with ongoing influence on both literature and social movements. ❀

# Plot Summary of
## *War and Peace*

Tolstoy described his purpose for writing *War and Peace*: "To love life in all its innumerable, inexhaustible manifestations"(Epilogue). He resisted calling it a novel because of its immense scope. "War" includes the vast domaine of public affairs—the activity of battlefield and diplomacy. "Peace" includes the uncountable family interactions occurring in familiar and beloved landscapes. The time period—Russian history between 1805 and 1820—covers Napoleon's imperial campaign against the Russian people including the battles of Austerlitz and Borodino and the burning of Moscow. Adding to the novel's originality are Tolstoy's blending the stories of historical with fictional characters and his double presence in the text—that of narrator and author who intermittently meditates on the events of his own story.

Getting into the world of *War and Peace* is like entering an Omni theatre: one is simultaneously confused and mesmerized by the multiplicity of events and the scope of the alternating landscapes. This disorientation reveals Tolstoy's obsession with truth and perspective, appearance and reality. Quickly enough, the reader becomes comfortable with the captivating and intermingled stories.

A few clarities facilitate the reader's way into the novel. Following the French Revolution (1787–1799) Napoleon engaged in years of empire building. The Battle of Austerlitz (Book Three) was a major victory. Alexander II continued Russian resistance, but, preferring peace, met with Napoleon at Tilsit (Book Five) to sign a treaty establishing separate powers over a divided Europe. The placated Napoleon expanded into other regions but returned in 1812 with his Grande Armee to invade an uncooperative Russia. The Battle of Borodino (Book Ten) ended indecisively with inhospitable weather and primitive medical care contributing to huge losses on both sides and incalculable suffering. A Russian rout (Book Thirteen) and an early severe winter inflicted heavy losses on the French. Russia prevailed by having, in effect, surrounded and swallowed her enemy. Napoleon's decline commenced.

Tolstoy loved Russia and expressed an intense interest in writing a psychological portrait of Napoleon and Alexander. Disagreeing with

Hegel's reverence for great public figures as determinants of history, Tolstoy believed history was the outcome of all the people alive at a certain time. Napoleon's invasion, Tolstoy thought, engendered a rise of Russian nationalist sentiment that became the occasion of uncountable small acts of courage, steadfastness, and compassion that constituted the beloved Russian soul.

In addition to the struggle between nations, Tolstoy wrote about the struggle between and within families. Three aristocratic families dominate the story along with Pierre who embraces so great a wealth of contradictory tendencies and insights that he touches indelibly all parts of the novel.

It is commonly observed that *War and Peace* lacks the traditional beginning, end, and climax—almost certainly intentional as Tolstoy believed this to be the condition of life—but he uses numerous contrasts that function as structure. Besides the great themes of war and peace there are the activities of battlefield and soiree; the European ethos of Petersburg and the old-fashioned patriarchal atmosphere of Moscow; the Russian ruling classes and the peasants; urban and rural poverty; epic and interior landscapes; and the confident war strategists trying to control the unruly battlefield. In addition, Tolstoy repeats phrases like "peculiar to" and "as is always the case" that reveal his prominent belief that each human being express both unique and inevitable aspects of human nature.

At least four themes animate and unite the novel: the meaning of history; the power of forgiveness and love; the mystery of evil; and the unceasing but impossible desire to understand life.

Tolstoy wrote *War and Peace* between 1864 and 1869. It was published in sections, appearing as a complete work in 1873. There are fifteen books and an Epilogue.

Two views of Russian society at peace fill **Book One.** The opening scene at Anna Pavlovna's soiree reveals the pretentions of upperclass Petersburg society. Prince Andrei joins the army to escape, and Pierre, awkward and newly arrived from Moscow, unnerves everyone by his social earnestness. The hostess manipulates conversations and all display the confidence of the ruling class. In contrast is family life. The Rostovs enjoy each other's company. The Bolkonskys at Bald Hills are emotionally strained between generations but loyal to each other. Illegitimate son Pierre attends the death of his father receiving both name and wealth and a suddenly elevated social status. Pierre can't decide if a look he exchanges with his father has extreme or no significance—a characteristic Tolstoy moment.

**Book Two** introduces the grimness, seductive appeal, and incongruity of war. Ill-equipped Russian soldiers are carried off battlefields in stretchers. Nikolay Rostov falls wounded under his dying horse and cannot comprehend why the French want to kill him—he so appealing and beloved—and flees to save his young life. Both valiance and disorder occur at the battle of Schongraben. In confusion, Russians shoot Austrians, their allies. Kutuzov, the Russian commander-in-chief is circumspect. Napoleon is bold and single-focused. The calm blue sky appears indifferent but the earth groans at the impact of a fallen cannonball.

Major changes befall Pierre and Prince Andrei in **Book Three**. In Petersburg, unsophisticated Pierre succumbs to the self-serving manipulations of Prince Vassily's circle and marries the "voluptuous, heartless" Helene. After valiantly carrying the flag at Austerlitz Prince Andrei finds himself lying wounded under the stars. Nearness of death and the infinite majesty of the sky combine to create an epiphany which reduces military glory to insignificance and Napoleon's words to the "buzzing of flies." Asking for mercy, Prince Andrei realizes he doesn't know whom he is addressing. From this moment until his death, Prince Andrei will know only the "nothingness . . . that is comprehensible . . . and the grandeur of [the] incomprehensible."

Another Tolstoy moment opens **Book Four**. Nikolay, with Denisov, home on leave, halts before the threshold, remembering the beloved crooked steps. The Rostov family reunion that begins when he opens the familiar door handle is boisterous, heartfelt, and prolonged. But there are also failed efforts. Natasha turns down Denisov's proposal; Helene has an affair with Dolokhov which draws a reluctant Pierre into an ineffectual duel and bafflement over his marriage; Sonia rejects Dolokhov after the duel because she loves Nikolay her "cousin"; Prince Andrei's wife dies in childbirth; and Nikolay and Dolokhov lose money at cards.

In **Book Five** following the duel Pierre falls into nihilism and behaves "as though the chief screw in his brain . . . [was] loose." In Petersburg he meets some "corpse-like travelers" who turn out to be Freemasons whose rational teachings temporarily capture his loyalty.

Princess Marya nurses her nephew, Nikolushka, Prince Andrei's son. Nikolay returns to battle finding the stench of death everywhere. Napoleon crushes Prussia and meets Alexander at Tilsit to make peace. Prince Andrei tells Pierre of his change of heart and plans to engage in the business of public reform.

**Book Six** is an interlude of peace. It begins in the burgeoning springtime of 1909 and introduces beautiful and ebullient Natasha Rostova as a young woman. Prince Andrei identifies morosely with an old leafless oak on his way to duties that bring him to the Rostov estate at Otradnoe. Natasha's irrepressible intoxication with life stirs Andrei who on return discovers that both he and the oak are in bloom. In a scene of remarkable family intimacy, Natasha and her mother discuss romantic details. At a ball Prince Andrei and Natasha fall in love. The marriage proposal thrills her but the year's delay imposed by old count Bolkonsky deflates her. Pierre, losing faith in Freemasonry, is accused of an obscure heresy. He draws away from Helene who holds pretentious intellectual soirees.

**Book Seven** is full of festivity and family harmony. Rostov siblings adore each other and their imaginative playfulness enlivens everyone. Natasha rides with her brother on the memorable wolf hunt and later enchants the family with her intuitive ability to perform traditional Russian dances. Dazzling sun and moonlight fall on the snow. The book ends with old count Rostov moving his family to Moscow to sell their house and make marriage arrangements.

In contrast, the mood of **Book Eight** is dark and chaotic. At the opera Natasha's dismay (a sign of "moral vibrancy") over the falsity of performed emotion and impatience with the marriage delay makes her vulnerable to the scheming Helene and she falls into a reckless affair with the rakish Anatole Kuragin. Overcome by tension and shame, Natasha takes arsenic. Prince Andrei releases her from commitment and Pierre reassures her that she has good life still ahead. As always, he is stirred by her presence. His metaphysical anxiety rises and he obsessively asks Tolstoy's own questions (What's the use? What for?) and ponders the incongruity of both Spain and France thanking the same Catholic God for victories over each other. Dread of coming war permeates the Book.

In **Book Nine** Tolstoy describes Napoleon's 1812 invasion of Russia: ". . . an event . . . opposed to human reason and all human nature." Pierre deciphers Biblical numbers and letters to conclude that Napoleon is the beast prophesied in the Apocalypse. Natasha prays for the enemy and forgiveness for all during the priest's prayer for deliverance of Russia from the same enemy. Tolstoy regarded compassion and the capacity for forgiveness—here embodied in Natasha—as the life-giving virtues that will save Russia.

**Book Ten** describes the ravages of war on the countryside and the Battle of Borodino. During Prince Andrei's effort to rescue Bleak Hills from enemy occupation he experiences an epiphany at the sight of two little girls courageously stealing some green plums: "He became aware of the existence of other human interests . . . remote from him, and as legitimate as his own." Later, fatally wounded, he forgives his former foe, Kuragin, also wounded. Tolstoy fills the Book with observations of the absurdity of war but sees as well war's capacity to generate profound human insights and relationships.

In **Book Eleven** a peasant child of six overhears a military strategy session and speaks for Tolstoy when she concludes that "'Granddad's' words [the intuitive Kutuzov] . . . put that 'Longcoat' [the rational general Bennigsen] down." Kutuzov's decision to retreat leaves Moscow in flames but also sets the conditions that lead to Russia's ultimate victory. Until he is captured by the French, Pierre wanders the burning streets crazed with confusion and a belief that he is ordained to kill Napoleon. Natasha implores her mother to abandon their belongings in the evacuating carriages to make room for the wounded—an example, Tolstoy says, of "the eggs teaching the hen." Natasha discovers Prince Andrei among them and they exchange forgiveness. Helene falls into deeper debauchery. Pierre saves a baby from the flames.

In the desperate period of **Book Twelve** between the loss of Moscow and the Russian rout Prince Andrei and Princess Helene die very different kinds of death. Prince Andrei achieves a visionary experience of universal love. The relationship of Nikolay Rostov and Princess Marya deepens. Pierre's escape from execution as an "incendiary" displays the delicate randomness of fate. In prison he befriends the peasant Platon Karataev who has befriended a dog. Eager and innocent Petya Rostov heads for battle.

Tolstoy states that it is not possible to find a single cause for the Russian turnaround—described in **Book Thirteen**—despite the innate human need to understand everything. Kutuzov's strength was to have kept Russian troops from useless fighting while the French weakened themselves by pillaging Moscow, leading to a reversal of fortune. Still a prisoner, Pierre, in the company of Karataev, experiences an inner freedom greater than anything he has known in his life.

In **Book Fourteen** "The people had a single aim: to clear their country of the invaders." During the rout Karataev dies and his dog companion howls. Compassionate and generous Petya gives his raisins to the frightened French drummer boy, and, impulsively riding against the French, is randomly shot and killed instantly just before the Russian prisoners are rescued. Carried by this sweep of emotion Pierre achieves a grateful oneness with life which comes from God's love.

**Book Fifteen** describes the final eviction of the French and the aftermath of war. The Rostov family is shattered by Petya's death; Natasha brings herself back to life by beckoning her mother away from death. Pierre learns of his wife's and Prince Andrei's deaths. He visits the newly married Princess Marya and Nikolay to share his grief over their family losses. While there he reconnects with Natasha so changed by the intervening years that he doesn't immediately recognize her. Moscow is rebuilt. The book ends in an unfinished sentence.

The two-part **Epilogue** extends Tolstoy's views on history, power, and free will and gives a picture of the domestic lives of Princess Marya and Nikolai, Pierre and Natasha—the next generation of Russian families. ❀

# List of Characters in
## *War and Peace*

The **Bolkonsky** family lives at Bald Hills. **Old Count Bolkonsky,** formerly a general in Catherine's reign, is eccentric, proud, and emotionally stiff. Inexplicably he torments **Princess Marya Bolkonsky** by ridiculing her studying, but a stroke leaves him asking for forgiveness. **Prince Andrei** carries the family's honor and commitment to public service. Always contemptuous of "imbecilic society" Prince Andrei prefers the action and valor of military life, but is transformed by the novel's events to a selfless understanding of universal love. The transformative events include his failed romance with Natasha and being wounded at Austerlitz. His "doll-like" wife **Princess Lise** dies in childbirth and Princess Marya takes over the care of her nephew little **Nikolai.** She is capable of seeing the "otherness" of people and her plain face radiates an inner beauty which draws many to her including Nikolay Rostov whom she marries.

The **Rostov** family resides at Otradnoe and Moscow. **Old Count Rostov** is a kindly, devoted father. He enjoys filling his house with guests who partake of the family's festive hospitality. As the patriarch he has been too generous and thus ineffectual in preserving the family wealth. When not trying to rein in her husband, **Countess Rostova** hovers protectively over the children to ensure their health and entry into wealthy marriages. Rostov siblings **Natasha** and **Nikolay** are especially memorable for their mutual adoration, inventive playfulness, and exuberance. Natasha has moments of irrepressible vitality and daring, possessing a rare ability to respond to life without self-consciousness. Love flows from her and intoxicates all in her presence. These qualities make possible deep personal growth enabling her later in life to respond instinctively in crises with compassion and forgiveness. Nikolay is essentially noble, alternately dreamy and earnest. Nikolay initially loves **Sonia** who lives as a ward of the family and adores him and Natasha especially. **Petya** the youngest, impulsive and always underfoot, is adored by all, and his unnecessary death by random gunshot is a grievous loss. The remaining Rostov children are more ordinary. **Natalya** is prudent and self-centered and **Vera's** frankness is unpleasant.

In contrast to the Bolkonsky and Rostov families who are essentially selfless and public-spirited, the **Kuragin** family is superficial and self-absorbed. Tolstoy called them "a brood of vipers." **Prince Vassily** is a pretentious courtier with a "perfumed bald head" who schemes to advance the fortunes of his children. **Princess Helene** has voluptuous beauty and no character. Her father snares Pierre into marrying her. Helene has affairs and holds pretentious soirees that alienate her husband. She dies—apparently a consequence of promiscuity. Brother **Anatole** is a handsome energetic playboy. He takes advantage of Natasha's vulnerable state, creating scandal and an end to her dignified betrothal to Prince Andrei. **Hyppolite** the younger brother, a striving diplomat, is astonishingly inept. **Julie** piously mourns the loss of a brother in Turkey.

**Pierre Bezukhov** is the illegitimate but favorite child of **Old Count Bezukov** who bestows his name and wealth at death. Pierre's soul is too large to be contained and he has trouble finding a place. He must act the part of a titled nobleman but his true nature is child-like and questioning. Sent to Prince Vassily for social polish he succumbs to Helene's charms and marries her—an act that chronically baffles him. Pierre wonders incessantly about life's meaning (even continuing to read while undressing) and experiences prolonged periods of despair. His brief enthusiasm for Freemasonry wanes when he finds it too rational and hypocritical, and his belief that his destiny is to kill Napoleon is similarly short-lived. Taken prisoner in Moscow, Pierre experiences an inner freedom so profound that he laughs at the notion that the fences the French have erected could ever contain him.

**Kutuzov** is Russia's unlikely commander-in-chief—old, bent over, and stout—who successfully prefers patience and intuition to elaborate military strategy to deliver his country.

**Denisov** is a zealous soldier and friend of Nikolay Rostov.

**Dolokhov,** a dissolute soldier, has an affair with Helene and is wounded in a duel with Pierre.

**Anna Pavlovna** holds soirees where members of Petersburg society talk about inconsequential things.

**Platon Karataev,** Pierre's companion in prison, is "everything Russian, kindly, and round." He possesses a gift for living—a capacity to love indiscriminately whatever is around—which he imparts to Pierre. When Karataev dies his dog companion howls. ❁

# Critical Views on
## *War and Peace*

I. S. TURGENEV ON *WAR AND PEACE*

[Turgenev, Russian writer (*Fathers and Sons*, 1862), presented Russian peasantry with realism and affection but differed from Tolstoy by taking a European outlook that encouraged Russia's move into a new age.]

[From a letter to P. P. Borisov, 16 March 1865]

... Since receiving your letter, I've succeeded in reading Ostrovsky's drama *Voevod* and the beginning of Tolstoy's novel. I am sincerely disappointed to admit that the novel strikes me as positively bad, boring, and unsuccessful. Tolstoy took a wrong turn and all his failings have become more obvious. All those little tricks, cunningly marked, and pretentiously put forth, those petty little psychological remarks, which he plucks out from the armpits and other dark places of his heroes and presents under the pretext of truth—how meager all that is on the broad canvas of a historical novel! And he puts this unfortunate product higher than *The Cossacks*! All the worse for him if he really means it. And how cold and dry everything is—how one feels the lack of imagination and the naïveté of the author, and how wearisome is the effect of a memory of so much that is petty, incidental, and useless. And what young ladies! All scrofulous and all putting on airs. No, one mustn't do it that way. That's going downhill, even with his talent. It pains me very much and I would enjoy being mistaken.

[From a letter to I. I. Borisov, 10 March 1868]

... I read Tolstoy's novel with pleasure, although I remain dissatisfied with a lot. The whole picture of military and daily life is done astonishingly well: There are things that will not die as long as the Russian language lives. But the whole *historical* side—forgive the expression—is a puppet show. Not to mention that there is no real reproduction of the times. What we learn about Alexander, Speransky, and others is only trifles, capriciously chosen by the author and put forth as characteristic traits. That's a form of charlatanism. ...

[From a letter to P. V. Annenkov, 13 April 1868]

I was sent Tolstoy's fourth volume. There is much that is fine, but you cannot overlook the deformities. It is a pity when an amateur, especially like Tolstoy, takes to philosophizing. He inevitably gets on some hobby horse, thinks up some system that settles everything right away, as for example, historical fatalism and starts to write. There where he touches the earth, like Antaeus, he gets back all his strength: the death of the old prince, Alpatych, the uprising in the village—all that is astonishingly well done. Natasha, though, comes out badly....

[From a letter to Tolstoy in which Turgenev is quoting from a letter to him from Flaubert, 12 January 1880]

Thanks for having me read Tolstoy's novel. It is first rate! What a painter and psychologist! The first two volumes are *sublime,* but the third goes downhill terribly. He repeats himself and he philosophizes. One sees finally the author and the Russian, and up to then one saw only *Nature* and *Humanity.* At times, it seemed to me there were things like Shakespeare's. I cried out in admiration while reading—but it is long!

—I. S. Turgenev, *Collected Works,* vol. 12 (Moscow, 1956). Trans. Edward Wasiolek, *Critical Essays on Tolstoy*, ed. Edward Wasiolek (Boston: G. K. Hall & Co., 1986): pp. 61–62.

## ANONYMOUS ON THE PUBLICATION OF *WAR AND PEACE* IN ENGLISH

With the appearance of the two compact volumes of the third part, Tolstoï's stupendous *War and Peace* at last is complete for English readers. The work is not new, it having been published first in Russian in 1860, and in French in 1884. Considered simply as an addition to recent English literature it is assuredly one of the most considerable events of the year—as important in its department as was the introduction to us of *Les Misérables.* ⟨...⟩

⟨. . .⟩ Much has already been said and more will continue to be said, in the heat of present enthusiasm, of Tolstoï the man, the moralist, the philosophical historian, the Christian communist. Before he has been thoroughly anatomized for the delectation of aesthetic criticism, there is yet a little space in which simple and healthy minds may rejoice over this fresh, strong vitality, which comes to us from that fascinating, because unknown, borderland of eastern and western civilization. Any translation is so welcome that we forbear to speak in particular of the failings of the present effort—though one has only to take the French version and find that in English *War and Peace* has been at times foully dealt with. Nevertheless, the worst second hand paraphrasing from Russian to French and from French to English cannot efface the brilliant effects of the original. And what pictures some of them are! The brutal bully Dologhow balanced on the lofty window-sill drinking off a bottle of rum for a trivial wager, the fascinating, weak, but really noble Pierre Besonkhow in his father's death room, the only honest soul there, the elopement of Natacha, the gleaming shoulders of Pierre's vile wife, those few awful seconds when Prince André speculated on the fateful shell which was to shatter him, the eternal calm of the peasant Platon, the most nearly perfect ideal of what Tolstoï now holds to! These and many more can never be forgotten, cannot even become dimmed in memory. Tolstoï's is no patent process in photography—it is rather the mirror of a river which suggests depths under its surface; the mirror truthfully reflects the objectivity of nature, but the reflection is subjective. It is much more than realism, for Tolstoï never could have come down so far as merely that. There are passages which to intelligences still unused to the savageries of an almost unintelligible semi-civilization must seem barbarous, but how different in all their sincerity from the horrors of such a book as *Salammbô*!

The chaos, the turbulence, the seeming incoherence of *War and Peace,* especially in the battle scenes, are felt to be like the unrest of life itself, even as the affairs of men and society appear to those who are in the mental condition in which Tolstoï found himself when he wrote. There are undoubtedly grave obstacles to those who decide to journey through this apparently fatalistic scheme of human existence; there are fair valleys and towering heights, but there are also *mauvaises terres,* wearisome perhaps beyond description, as there are in the course of daily life. This, then, is Tolstoï's accomplishment, the revivification, as it were, of humanity as it existed in Russia before and during the invasion of Napoleon.

—Anonymous, *Literary World,* trans. Clara Bell. (1886): pp. 348–49.

## N. N. Strakhov on Tolstoy's Success as a Realist

[Strakhov, editor and critic, was a friend of Tolstoy. Writing in 1895 Strakhov claimed that the popular success of *War and Peace* was not attributable to any contrived sensationalism but rather to an abundance of realistic psychological detail from everyday life.]

⟨. . .⟩ Nothing could be simpler than the multitude of events depicted in *War and Peace.* All events of ordinary family life, conversations between brother and sister, mother and daughter, separation and reunion of kinfolk, the hunt, the celebration of Christmas and New Years, the mazurka, the card game, and so forth; all of this is made into a pearl of creation with the same love that went into the description of the Borodino battle. ⟨. . .⟩

⟨. . .⟩ One would be hard pressed to visualize images more sharp, colors more vivid. It is as if one were to see with one's own eyes all that is being described, to hear the sounds of all that is going on. The author tells nothing from his own point of view: he directly brings out persons and makes them speak, feel, and act, whereby every word and every movement rings true to an amazingly accurate degree, that is, it fully bears the character of the person to whom it belongs. It is as if one were to deal with living people and see them much more clearly than one is able to see in real life. One can discern not only the modes of expression and feelings that distinguish every protagonist, but even his mannerisms, favorite gestures, his gait. ⟨. . .⟩

⟨. . .⟩ Tolstoy has no images or descriptions made from his own point of view. Nature appears only in the way it is reflected in the actions of the protagonists; he does not describe the oak that stands in the middle of the path, or the moonlit night during which Natasha and Prince Andrei were unable to sleep but describes the impression this oak and this night made upon Prince Andrei. Just so, battles and happenings of all kinds are told not according to the conceptions formed about them by the author but according to the impressions of people who participated in them. The Schoengraben action is described mostly on the basis of Prince Andrei's impressions; the battle of Austerlitz on the basis of Nikolai Rostov's impressions; the arrival of Emperor Alexander in Moscow is reflected in Petja's excitement, and the effect of the prayer to save Russia from the invasion is depicted in Natasha's feelings. In this way, the author nowhere appears from behind his protagonists, and depicts events not in abstractions but with the flesh and blood of those people who contributed materially to the events. ⟨. . .⟩

⟨T⟩he outstanding feature of Tolstoy's talent ⟨is⟩ his ability to depict the movements within the psyche with extraordinary accuracy and precision. One might call Tolstoy primarily a *psychological realist*. He has made a reputation for himself in his previous works as an amazing master in the skill of analyzing all kinds of psychological changes and conditions. ⟨. . .⟩

⟨An example is the relationship between the Old Count and his daughter Princess Marya.⟩ ⟨I⟩t seems impossible to forgive the old man for the suffering his daughter has to endure from him. Of all the personages depicted by the artist, no one, apparently, deserves greater condemnation. But then, what is the situation? With consummate skill, the author has depicted for us one of the worst and most pathetic human frailties—one that is impervious to assault by either mind or will—and one that deserves our most sincere pity. Actually the old man is dissolved in boundless devotion to his daughter—he literally *cannot live without her*; but this love has become perverted in his heart into a desire to inflict pain upon himself and his love object. He is constantly tugging at this inseparable bond that links him to his daughter, and in so doing, finds morbid pleasure in *such* feeling of being bound to her. All shadings of this strange relationship are caught by Tolstoy with incredible accuracy and the denouement—when the old man, broken by illness and near death, expresses at last all his tenderness for his daughter—makes a profoundly moving impression.

The strongest, purest feeling can be perverted to such a degree! People can inflict upon themselves such suffering through their own fault! One can hardly imagine a picture that would prove more conclusively that man is sometimes totally unable to control himself. The relations between the dignified old man Bolkonsky and his son and daughter, based in a jealous and perverted sense of love represent that evil, which often is found in intimate family relationships, and proves to us that the holiest and most natural feelings can acquire an insane and savage character.

Nevertheless, these feelings are at the root of the matter, and their perversion must not hide from us their pure source. And during a shattering experience, their true nature often comes fully to the fore: in dying, old Bolkonsky is overwhelmed by love for his daughter.

To see what is hidden in the soul of man under the play of passions, under all forms of selfishness, greed, animal desires—this is what Tolstoy knows how to do brilliantly. ⟨...⟩

> —N. N. Strakhov, *Critical Articles about I. S. Turgenev and L. N. Tolstoy, 1862–1885,* 3rd edition, (St. Petersburg, 1895). Trans. Boris Sorokin, *Critical Essays on Tolstoy,* ed. Edward Wasiolek, (Boston: G. K. Hall & Co., 1986): pp. 75–82.

## V. I. Lenin on Tolstoy's Contribution to Russia and the Revolution

[V. I. Lenin, founder of the Russian Communist Party, was arrested as a subversive in 1895 and sent to Siberia. Returning to Russia he led the Bolshevik revolution in 1917. Tolstoy's subject was history but in the end what mattered was the unfolding of individual lives within that history. Lenin's subject was revolution by the peasant proletariat. This contrast is highlighted in Lenin's praise for the writer and criticism of the teaching.]

The contradictions in the works, views, doctrines, the school of Tolstoy are glaring indeed. On the one hand we have the brilliant artist who has produced not only incomparable pictures of Russian life but also first-rate works of world literature. On the other hand we have a country squire acting the fool-in-Christ. On the one hand we have a remarkably powerful, direct, and sincere protest against social lies and falsehood, while on the other we have the "Tolstoyan," i.e., the washed-out hysterical sniveller, a gutless species known as the Russian intellectual who publicly beats his breast and cries: "I am vile, I am disgusting, but I am working on my own moral self-improvement: I no longer eat meat and nourish myself with rice patties." On the one hand Tolstoy remorselessly criticizes capitalist exploitation and exposes the violent methods of the government, the farce of the courts and of public administration, reveals the entire extent of the contradictions between the growth of wealth and the achievements of civilization, and the increasing destitution, brutalization, and misery of the working masses; on the other he preaches his feeble-minded doctrine of "nonreselessly to evil" by forceful means. On the one hand there is the most sober realism of his works, the tearing away of all and sundry masks; on the other he preaches one of the vilest things on earth—religion—and wants to replace priests who look upon their job as an official function with priests who would do the same from moral conviction, that is, he promotes the far subtler and therefore particularly repulsive form of clericalism. Indeed [one could say with the poet Nekrasov]:

> Indigent and abundant,
> Mighty and impotent
> Is Mother Russia.

It is self-evident that Tolstoy, given such contradictions, could not possibly understand either the labor movement and its role in the struggle for socialism, or the Russian revolution. ⟨. . .⟩ Tolstoy is ridiculous as a prophet who has discovered new prescriptions for the salvation of mankind, and therefore utterly ridiculous are those miserable foreign and Russian "Tolstoyans" who have attempted to make a dogma out of the weakest side of his doctrine. But Tolstoy is great as the spokesman of the ideas and moods that arose among millions of Russian peasants at the time when the bourgeois revolution arrived in Russia. ⟨. . .⟩

Tolstoy['s works] reflect the pent-up hatred, the ripened desire for a better life, the desire to get rid of the past, as well as the immature dreaming, lack of political skills, and revolutionary spinelessness [of the peasantry]. Historical and economic conditions explain both the inevitability of the beginning revolutionary struggle within the masses, as well as their lack of preparedness for this struggle, their

Tolstoyan nonresistance to evil, which was a most serious cause of the defeat of the first revolutionary campaign [of 1905].

—V. I. Lenin, "Leo Tolstoy as the Mirror of the Russian Revolution," *Proletariat* 35 (1908), trans. Boris Sorokin, *Critical Essays on Tolstoy*, ed. Edward Wasiolek (Boston: G. K. Hall & Co., 1983): pp. 20–21, 23.

## PERCY LUBBOCK ON THE NOVEL'S FORMLESSNESS

[Percy Lubbock was an English writer who wrote about Henry James, Edith Wharton, and Elizabeth Barrett Browning. He is prominent among Tolstoy's admirers who assert that the novel has no discernible structure.]

Of *War and Peace* it has never been suggested, I suppose, that Tolstoy here produced a model of perfect form. It is a panoramic vision of people and places, a huge expanse in which armies are marshalled; can one expect of such a book that it should be neatly composed? It is crowded with life, at whatever point we face it; intensely vivid, inexhaustibly stirring, the broad impression is made by the big prodigality of Tolstoy's invention. If a novel could really be as large as life, Tolstoy could easily fill it; his great masterful reach never seems near its limit; he is always ready to annex another and yet another tract of life, he is only restrained by the mere necessity of bringing a novel somewhere to an end. ⟨...⟩

⟨...⟩ Tolstoy *seems* to know precisely where he is going, and why; there is nothing at any moment to suggest that he is not in perfect and serene control of his idea. Only at last, perhaps, we turn back and wonder what it was. What is the subject of *War and Peace,* what is the novel *about*? There is no very ready answer; but if we are to discover what is wrong with the form, this is the question to press. ⟨...⟩

The long, slow, steady sweep of the story—the *first* story, as I call it—setting through the personal lives of a few young people, bringing them together, separating them, dimming their freshness, carrying them away from hopeful adventure to their appointed condition, where their part is only to transmit the gift of youth to others and to drop back while the adventure is repeated—this motive, in with the book opens and closes and to which it constantly returns, is broken into by the famous scenes of battle ⟨...⟩ with the reverberation of imperial destinies, out of which Tolstoy makes a saga of his country's tempestuous past. It is magnificent, this latter, but it has no bearing on the other, the universal story of no time or country, the legend of every age, which is told of Nicholas and Natasha, but which might have been told as well of the sons and daughters of the king of Troy. To Nicholas, the youth of all time, the strife of Emperor and Czar is the occasion, it may very well be, of the climax of his adventure; ⟨...⟩ but if it is *his* story, his and that of his companions, why do we see them suddenly swept into the background, among the figures that populate the story of a particular and memorable war? For that is what happens. ⟨...⟩

Tolstoy's novel is wasteful of its subject; that is the whole objection to its loose, unstructural form. Criticism bases its conclusion upon nothing whatever but the injury done to the story, the loss of its full potential value. Is there so much that is good in *War and Peace* that its inadequate grasp of a great theme is easily forgotten? It is not only easily forgotten, it is scarcely noticed—on a first reading of the book; I speak at least for one reader. But with every return to it the book that *might* have been is more insistent; it obtrudes more plainly, each time, interfering with the book that is. Each time, in fact, it becomes harder to make a book of it at all; instead of holding together more firmly, with every successive reconstruction, its prodigious members seem always more disparate and disorganized; they will not coalesce. A subject, one and whole and irreducible—a novel cannot begin to take shape till it has this for its support.

—Percy Lubbock, *Critical Essays on Tolstoy,* ed. Edward Wasiolek (Boston: G. K. Hall & Co.,1986) pp. 92, 93, 95–96, 99.

[Virginia Woolf, English author of *To the Lighthouse* (1927) and *A Room of One's Own* (1929), singles out Tolstoy's famous question—Why Live?—and discusses the way his characters are measured by their response.]

There remains the greatest of all novelists—for what else can we call the author of *War and Peace*? Shall we find Tolstoi, too, alien, difficult, a foreigner? Is there some oddity in his angle of vision which, at any rate until we have become disciples and so lost our bearings, keeps us at arm's length in suspicion and bewilderment? From his first words we can be sure of one thing at any rate—here is a man who sees what we see, who proceeds, too, as we are accustomed to proceed, not from the inside outwards, but from the outside inwards. Here is a world in which the postman's knock is heard at eight o'clock, and people go to bed between ten and eleven. Here is a man, too, who is no savage, no child of nature; he is educated; he has had every sort of experience. He is one of those born aristocrats who have used their privileges to the full. He is metropolitan, not suburban. His senses, his intellect, are acute, powerful, and well nourished. There is something proud and superb in the attack of such a mind and such a body upon life. Nothing seems to escape him. Nothing glances off him unrecorded. Nobody, therefore, can so convey the excitement of sport, the beauty of horses, and all the fierce desirability of the world to the senses of a strong young man. Every twig, every feather sticks to his magnet. He notices the blue or red of a child's frock; the way a horse shifts its tail; the sound of a cough; the action of a man trying to put his hands into pockets that have been sewn up. And what his infallible eye reports of a cough or a trick of the hands his infallible brain refers to something hidden in the character so that we know his people, not only by the way they love and their views on politics and the immortality of the soul, but also by the way they sneeze and choke. Even in a translation we feel that we have been set on a mountain-top and had a telescope put into our hands. Everything is astonishingly clear and absolutely sharp. ⟨. . .⟩ But always there is an element of fear which makes us ⟨. . .⟩ wish to escape from the gaze which Tolstoi fixes on us. Does it arise from the sense, which in real life might harass us, that such happiness as he describes is too intense to last, that we are on the edge of disaster? Or is it not that the very intensity of our pleasure is somehow questionable and forces us to ask, with Pozdnyshev in the Kreutzer Sonata, "But why live?" Life dominates Tolstoi as the soul dominates Dostoevsky. There is always at the centre of all the brilliant and flashing petals of the flower this scorpion, "Why live?" There is always at the centre of the book some Olenin, or Pierre, or Levin who gathers into himself all experience, turns the world round between his fingers, and never ceases to ask even as he enjoys it, what is the meaning of it, and what should be our aims. It is not the priest who shatters our desires most effectively; it is the man who has known them, and loved them himself. When he derides them, the world indeed turns to dust and ashes beneath our feet. Thus fear mingles with our pleasure, and of three great Russian writers, it is Tolstoi who most enthralls us and most repels.

—Virginia Woolf, *The Common Reader* (New York: Harcourt, Brace, 1925): pp. 253–56.

## G. K. Chesterton on Tolstoy the Man

[G. K. Chesterton, the English writer and defender of Orthodoxy contributes in this tiny book on Tolstoy a novel understanding of his greatness.]

If any one wishes to form the fullest estimate of the real character and influence of the great man whose name is prefixed to these remarks, he will not find it in his novels, splendid as they are, or in his ethical views, clearly and finely as they are conceived and expanded. He will find it best expressed in the news that has recently come from Canada, that a sect of Russian Christian anarchists has turned all its animals loose, on the ground that it is immoral to possess them or control them. About such an incident as this there is a quality altogether independent of the rightness or wrongness, the sanity or insanity, of the view. It is first and foremost a reminder that the world is still young. There are still theories of life as insanely reasonable as those which were disputed under the clear blue skies of Athens. There are still examples of a faith as fierce and practical as that of the Mahometans, who swept across Africa and Europe, shouting a single word. To the languid contemporary politician and philosopher it seems doubtless like something out of a dream, that in this iron-bound, homogeneous. and clockwork age, a company of European men in boots and waistcoats should begin to insist on taking the horse out of the shafts of the omnibus, and lift the pig out of his pig-sty, and the dog out of his kennel, because of a moral scruple or theory. It is like a page from some fairy farce to imagine the Doukhabor solemnly escorting a hen to the door of the yard and bidding it a benevolent farewell as it sets out on its travels. All this, as I say, seems mere muddle-headed absurdity to the typical leader of human society in this decade, to a man like Mr. Balfour, or Mr. Wyndham. But there is nevertheless a further thing to be said, and that is that, if Mr. Balfour could be converted to a religion which taught him that he was morally bound to walk into the House of Commons on his hands, and he did walk on his hands, if Mr. Wyndham could accept a creed which taught that he ought to dye his hair blue, and he did dye his hair blue, they would both of them be, almost beyond description, better and happier men than they are. For there is only one happiness possible or conceivable under the sun, and that is enthusiasm—that strange and splendid word that has passed through so many vicissitudes, which meant, in the eighteenth century the condition of a lunatic, and in ancient Greece the presence of a god.

⟨. . .⟩ Tolstoy, besides being a magnificent novelist, is one of the very few men alive who have a real, solid, and serious view of life. He is a Catholic church, of which he is the only member, the somewhat arrogant Pope and the somewhat submissive layman. He is one of the two or three men in Europe, who have an attitude towards things so entirely their own, that we could supply their inevitable view on anything—a silk hat, a Home Rule Bill, an Indian poem, or a pound of tobacco. ⟨. . .⟩ Tolstoy would say: "I believe in the utmost possible simplification of life; therefore, this silk hat is a black abortion." He would say: "I believe in the utmost possible simplification of life; therefore, this Home Rule Bill is a mere peddling compromise; it is no good to break up a centralised empire into nations, you must break the nation up into individuals." He would say: "I believe in the utmost possible simplification of life; therefore, I am interested in this Indian poem, for Eastern ethics, under all their apparent gorgeousness, are far simpler and more Tolstoyan than Western." He would say: "I believe in the utmost possible simplification of life; therefore, this pound of tobacco is a thing of evil; take it away."

Everything in the world, from the Bible to a bootjack, can be, and is, reduced by Tolstoy to this great fundamental Tolstoyan principle, the simplification of life. When we deal with a body of opinion like this we are dealing with an incident in the history of Europe infinitely more important than the appearance of Napoleon Buonaparte.

—G. K. Chesterton and G. H. Perris, *Leo Tolstoy* (New York: James Patt and Company; London: Hodder and Stoughton, no date): pp. 1–4.

## James T. Farrell on Tolstoy's Moral Panorama

[James T. Farrell was an American critic and novelist best known for *Studs Lonigan* (1935). In his study of literature as a reflection of a specific morality in contrast to a writer's effort to press upon readers a new morality, J. T. Farrell makes prominent use of *War and Peace* as an illustration of the latter. This extract offers his overview of the novel.]

Leo Tolstoy's *War and Peace* offers a panoramic portrait of the Tsarist feudal nobility during the Napoleonic period; it is a thoroughgoing depiction of the life of a whole social class, a class picture drawn in characterizations rather than by conceptualization. The Tsarist feudal nobility is presented in an amazing succession of sharply individualized and vigorously contrasted figures thrown against a historic background of war and peace.

The novel opens in one of the aristocratic drawing rooms of St. Petersburg in 1805, when Russia is at peace. We are introduced to some of those in the highest circles of a confident, self-assured ruling class which is still master of its country. The influential lady, Anna Pavlovna, reflects this assurance when she remarks: "Russia alone is to be the saviour of Europe. . . . Our good and sublime emperor has the greatest part in the world to play, and he is so virtuous and noble that God will not desert him, and he will fulfill his mission—to strangle the hydra of revolution." Revolution is personified in a "murderer and miscreant" named Napoleon Bonaparte.

These people do not feel that their Alexander will be a Louis XVI, nor that theirs will be the destiny of the French nobility. ⟨. . .⟩ This is a *ruling* class! It accepts its status as if by divine appointment. This society is cemented with the principle of authority, of autocracy, embodied in the youthful flesh and figure of the almost unapproachable Tsar, Alexander I. ⟨. . .⟩

In general, the social relationships of the life of this class are not conducive to moral and intellectual seriousness. In most instances, the antipathies among the characters are of a personal nature, caused by personal offenses, rivalries in love, rivalries in the quest for position, and differences in social status. In fact, personal antipathies involving the social code of honor can produce so serious a consequence as a duel; intellectual differences, however, even on fundamental political and moral questions, have much less serious consequences. Despite the fact that the narrative records terrible sufferings, catastrophic events, an invasion of Russia which almost destroys the very foundations of feudal absolutism, only a few of the characters—most notably Pierre and Prince Andrey—think in such a way that they can draw lessons from experience. And what is important, those characters who do think, think about themselves, their own moral problems, and the question of the moral ends of life. In other words, the real thinking is in terms of questions posed as a result of the historic rise of individualism in the West, and the reign of individualism in a moral and personal, as well as an economic sense, is a result of the Great French Revolution. Moral individualism is a central motif of *War and Peace*. ⟨. . .⟩

The almost miraculous class portrait is drawn by the creation of individual living human beings. And these human beings are given a place, a role in a work written, not from the perspective of private lives, but rather from that of history. They are seen not only as persons pursuing their own ends with the conviction that they freely will their actions but also as victims trapped and engulfed in one of the bloodiest and most irrepressible tides in human history.

—James T. Farrell, *Literature and Morality* (New York: Vanguard Press, Inc., 1945): pp. 185–186, 188, 190.

# Isaiah Berlin on Tolstoy's View of History

[Isaiah Berlin was a Latvian educated at Oxford who wrote on history, biography, and philosophy. In this extract Berlin clarifies Tolstoy's important view of history in *War and Peace*.]

Tolstoy's central thesis—in some respects not unlike the theory of the inevitable "self-deception" of the *bourgeoisie* held by his contemporary Karl Marx, save that what Marx reserves for a class, Tolstoy sees in almost all mankind—is that there is a natural law whereby the lives of human beings no less than those of nature are determined; but that men, unable to face this inexorable process, seek to represent it as a succession of free choices, to fix responsibility for what occurs upon persons endowed by them with heroic virtues or heroic vices, and called by them "great men." What are great men? they are ordinary human beings, who are ignorant and vain enough to accept responsibility for the life of society, individuals who would rather take the blame for all the cruelties, injustices, disasters justified in their name, than recognize their own insignificance and impotence in the cosmic flow which pursues its course irrespective of their wills and ideals. This is the central point of those passages (in which Tolstoy excelled) in which the actual course of events is described, side by side with the absurd, egocentric explanations which persons blown up with the sense of their own importance necessarily give to them; as well as of the wonderful descriptions of moments of illumination in which the truth about the human condition dawns upon those who have the humility to recognize their own unimportance and irrelevance. ⟨. . .⟩ There is a particularly vivid simile in which the great man is likened to the ram whom the shepherd is fattening for slaughter. Because the ram duly grows fatter, and perhaps is used as a bell-wether for the rest of the flock, he may easily imagine that he is the leader of the flock, and that the other sheep go where they go solely in obedience to his will. He thinks this and the flock may think it too. Nevertheless the purpose of his selection is not the role he believes himself to play, but slaughter—a purpose conceived by beings whose aims neither he nor the other sheep can fathom. For Tolstoy, Napoleon is just such a ram, and so to some degree is Alexander, and indeed all the great men of history.

⟨. . .⟩ Sometimes ⟨. . .⟩ Tolstoy vacillates; the individual is "in some sense" free when he alone is involved: thus in raising his arm, he is free within physical limits. But once he is involved in relationships with others, he is no longer free, he is part of the inexorable stream. Freedom is real, but it is confined to trivial acts. At other times even this feeble ray of hope is extinguished: Tolstoy declares that he cannot admit even small exceptions to the universal law; causal determinism is either wholly pervasive or it is nothing, and chaos reigns. Men's acts may seem free of the social nexus, but they are not free, they cannot be free, they are part of it. ⟨. . .⟩

It is not a mystical or an intuitionist view of life. Our ignorance of how things happen is not due to some inherent inaccessibility of the first causes, only to their multiplicity, the smallness of the ultimate units, and our own inability to see and hear and remember and record and co-ordinate enough of the available material. Omniscience is in principle possible even to empirical beings, but, of course, in practice unattainable. This alone, and nothing deeper or more interesting, is the source of human megalomania, of all our absurd delusions. Since we are not, in fact, free, but could not live without the conviction that we are, what are we to do? Tolstoy arrives at no clear conclusion, only at the view, in some respect like Burke's, that it is better to realize that we understand what goes on as we do in fact understand it—much as spontaneous, normal, simple people, uncorrupted by theories, not blinded by the dust raised by the scientific authorities, do, in fact, understand life—than to seek to subvert such common-sense beliefs, which at least have the merit of having been tested by long experience, in favour of pseudo-sciences, which, being founded on absurdly inadequate data, are only a snare and a delusion. That is his case against all forms of optimistic rationalism, the natural sciences, liberal theories of progress, German military *expertise,* French sociology, confident social engineering of all kinds.

—Isaiah Berlin, *The Hedgehog and the Fox* (New York: Mentor, 1957): pp. 28–51.

# ALBERT COOK ON REVELATION OF MORAL CHARACTER

[Albert Cook was a literary critic and professor of English at the University of New York at Buffalo and Brown University. Here, Cook particularizes an aspect of Tolstoy's theme and suggests ways it will animate the entire novel.]

Each original novelist, by virtue of the uniqueness of the world he creates, has a distinct kind of moral observation. We find that Hemingway analyzes the moral gestures of courage, Trollope of sincerity, Jane Austen of altruistic social insight, Defoe of economic and sexual scruple, Stendhal of crassness or fineness.

Tolstoy's world, for all its breadth, is no less single in its moral outlook. ⟨. . .⟩

The meaning of *War and Peace* is, however large, single and coherent. It creates its characters and builds its panoramic universe of moral meaning out of a sequence of observed and analyzed moral gestures:

> Prince Vassily always spoke languidly, like an actor repeating his part in an old play. Anna Pavlovna Scherer, in spite of her forty years, was on the contrary brimming over with excitement and impulsiveness. To be enthusiastic had become her pose in society, and at times even when she had, indeed, no inclination to be so, she was enthusiastic so as not to disappoint the expectations of those who knew her. ⟨. . .⟩

The surface of social life in the *soirée* of this chapter is presented as a kind of play. Most prominent are the most acting, the most hypocritical (Greek, actors); there are moving at the same time shyly and clumsily in the background, of this scene as throughout Book One, those dedicated beings we will come to know as the agents of a real moral life. Not that they yet know to what they are dedicated. Prince Vassily and Anna Pavlovna know; but their knowledge is not a true superiority; as here rendered, it is only the superficial skill of the actor. Their limit is that they know all they are to do; so they have chosen it.

In the keen individuation of Tolstoy's moral analysis, these two hypocrites are distinguished from one another: Prince Vassily is languid, Anna Pavlovna "brimming over with excitement and impulsiveness." These traits in turn are subjected to analysis. Every nuance of behavior undergoes a moral scrutiny.

What is the domain of Tolstoy's analysis? It is so perfectly fused with the theme of the novel that a short definition is not possible, but, roughly, he is always analyzing a character's attitude toward his own destiny, his own tempo, his own potentialities. Gesture always has become or is becoming moral habit in Tolstoy. He analyzes the certitude of the become, the hesitance of the becoming. Habit is subjected to time, transmuted and retransmuted, in a number of ways whose diversity his moral analysis renders, whose underlying interdependence the plot coordinates. The plot's grand scale of social process changes each phase's moral appearance into a new reality. To keep up with the times, with Time, to be morally real, a character must meet a challenge which faces everyone equally as it faces each at his own individual angle. What makes Anna Pavlovna Scherer and Prince Vassily superficial is their dedication to surface, implied in the meaning Tolstoy analyzes into their almost ritual gestures. Oriented toward mere appearance, they commit themselves toward their temporary social masks. This commitment affords them a certain adroitness, but it cuts them out of all the profounder resurrections of the years to come. Nine years and a thousand pages later the bumbling Pierre of the first scene of the novel will have become spiritually baptized and re-baptized into a moral giant. But Anna Pavlovna, withdrawn from the horribly contrasting background of devastated Moscow, will be giving the identical Petersburg *soirée,* politely and coldly ignoring the cataclysm that is to be the death through which the best will be reborn. And who is her honored guest but the same Prince Vassily, unchanged in his diabolical superficiality.

—Albert Cook, *The Moral Vision: Tolstoy The Meaning of Fiction* (Detroit: Wayne State University Press, 1960).

## R. F. CHRISTIAN ON CHARACTERIZATION

[R. F. Christian was professor of Russian at St. Andrew's University. In *Tolstoy's 'War and Peace'* he discusses Tolstoy's exceptionally memorable characters.]

Tolstoy's technique is to show that at every stage in the life of his heroes the likelihood of change is always present, so that at no time are they static, apathetic or inert, but constantly liable to respond to some new external or internal stimulus. Very often the stimulus is provided by a person from the opposite camp—a 'negative' character, a selfish, complacent or *static* man or woman. These people act as temptations to the heroes; they are obstacles in their path which have to be overcome. Pierre, for example, is momentarily blinded by the apparent greatness of Napoleon. He is trapped into marriage with Hélène, with whom he has nothing in common, and is in danger of being drawn into the Kuragin net. After their separation he is reconciled with her again, only to bemoan his fate once more as a retired gentleman-in-waiting, a member of the Moscow English Club and a universal favourite in Moscow society. Prince Andrei, like Pierre, is deceived by the symbol of Napoleon, and like Pierre he finds himself married to a woman who is as much his intellectual inferior as Hélène is morally beneath Pierre. Natasha for her part is attracted at first by the social climber Boris Drubetskoy and later infatuated by the same Anatole Kuragin who had actually begun to turn Princess Marya's head. Julie Karagina looms for a while on Nikolai's horizon. From all these temptations and involvements the heroes and heroines are saved, not by their own efforts but by the timely workings of Providence. Prince Andrei's wife dies. Pierre is provoked by Dolokhov into separating from his wife, and after their reconciliation he is eventually released by Hélène's death. Natasha is saved from herself by the solicitude of her friends. By chance Princess Marya catches Anatole unawares as he flirts with Mlle Bouricnne. (Nikolai, to his credit, is never likely to obey his mother's wishes and marry Julie.) It seems as if fate is working to rescue them from the clutches of egocentricity. But it is not only external circumstances such as personal associations with people of the opposite camp which are a challenge to Tolstoy's heroes and heroines. There are internal obstacles against which they have to contend, without any help from Providence. Tolstoy made it a main object of his characterization to show his positive heroes at all important moments 'becoming' and not just 'being', beset with doubts, tormented by decisions, the victims of ambivalent thoughts and emotions, eternally restless. As a result, their mobility, fluidity and receptivity to change are constantly in evidence, as they face their inner problems. Princess Marya has to overcome her instinctive aversion to Natasha. Nikolai has to wage a struggle between love and duty until he finds in the end that they can both be reconciled in one and the same person. Pierre's inner disquiet and spiritual striving express his determination, now weak, now strong, to overcome in himself the very qualities of selfishness and laziness which he despises in other people. Outward and inward pressures are continually being exerted on Pierre, Prince Andrei, Princess Marya, Natasha and Nikolai, and their lives are lived in a state of flux.

—R. F. Christian, *Tolstoy's 'War and Peace'* (London: Oxford University Press, 1962): pp. 172–173.

## Ernest J. Simmons on Characterization

[Ernest J. Simmons wrote extensively on Russian authors, including *Introduction to Russian Realism* (1965). He taught at Harvard, Cornell, and Columbia and was a member of the cultural commission to the USSR for the American Council of Learned Societies. Tolstoy's characters continue to dwell vividly in the reader's memory. Simmons offers additional explanation for this feature of Tolstoy.]

Tolstoy's techniques in characterization are part of the secret of his extraordinary realism, for one of the most difficult things for a novelist is to reveal the total personality of a character, as a person in real life reveals himself. The revelation of personality in real life comes about over a period of time by slow accretions, by the accumulation of much detailed information and understanding through innumerable small actions and intimacies. This is the logical, the natural way, and a close approximation of it is pursued in Tolstoy's novels. ⟨. . .⟩

Tolstoy does not confront us at the outset with the familiar lengthy description of a character, nor does he take refuge in the awkward flashback. We are introduced to Prince Andrew, Pierre, Natasha, or Nicholas in a customary setting, as we might be in the case of a future friend in real life. Our first impression of the external appearance is only that which we would see ourselves, conveyed by the author's few brief descriptive sentences. We learn next to nothing of the character's past or personality at this point. But from the reactions and remarks of others—this indirect method is a favorite of Tolstoy—and eventually through the conversation, self-examination, behavior, and actions of the character, spread out over many pages and years, our knowledge of him grows until finally we obtain a complete image. There are no startling or abrupt revelations. Each thought or emotion develops out of another. And in the case of characters with a pronounced moral and spiritual bent, like Prince Andrew and Pierre, their dissatisfaction with life is resolved, if ever, not by the author's philosophizing, but by a combination of prolonged self-examination, reflection, and extensive experiences on the part of the characters. ⟨. . .⟩ ⟨T⟩hese men and women never inhabit a world of their own, they seem to inhabit our world. That is, their world never strikes us as an abstract one. They stand forth fully defined with all their limitations of time, place, and circumstance. Tolstoy does not hover over the destinies of his men and women; they appear to exercise free choice in working out their fate, so that what they do seems to be psychologically necessary, even though their consciousness of freedom, in the Tolstoyan sense, is illusory. His psychological insights, like his style, create in the reader a sense of intimacy with the characters, for in his analysis of thoughts, feelings, and actions Tolstoy's points of reference are nearly always the reality of life and not abstractions. "You can invent anything you please," he once said of Gorky's fiction, "but it is impossible to invent psychology. . . ."

Such an approach goes beyond conventional realism and suggests not only Tolstoy's complete identification with his characters, but a genuine love for them. Even in negative characters, he nearly always discovers some good, which was his abiding principle in real life. The reprehensible Dolokhov is tenderly devoted to his mother, and the obnoxious Anatole Kuragin is apparently a brave officer in combat. The artist, Tolstoy believed, is called upon to portray his men and women, not to judge them. It almost seems as though he lived among the characters he created very much as he wanted to live among his friends and neighbors. "The best way to obtain true happiness," he wrote in his diary, "is, without any rules, to throw out from oneself on all sides, like a spider, an adhesive web of love to catch in it all that comes: an old woman, a child, a girl, or a policeman."

> —Ernest J. Simmons, *Introduction to Tolstoy's Writings* (Chicago: University of Chicago Press, 1968): pp. 77–79.

## E. B. GREENWOOD ON HOMERIC AND CHRISTIAN INFLUENCES ON TOLSTOY

[Tolstoy embraced competing concerns and influences. In his chapter "The Problem of Truth in *War and Peace*" E. B. Greenwood discusses two world views that held for Tolstoy an irreconcilable appeal and raised for him the universal question of the origin of evil.]

On 25 August 1857 ⟨Tolstoy⟩ wrote in his diary:

> Finished reading the incredibly delightful conclusion of the *Iliad* . . . After the *Iliad* read the Gospels, which I have not done for a long time. How could Homer not know that goodness is love! It was a revelation.

This passage focuses the 'clash of ideals' very clearly. Tolstoy was so impressed by Homer that, after he had finished *War and Peace*, he started to learn Greek in order to appreciate him more fully. I think there is a lot in Aylmer Maude's suggestion that the intense melancholy which overcame him about that time owed some of its force to the powerful opposition between two rival views of life which were both immensely attractive to him: the view of Homer and the view of Jesus. Three decades later, when he wrote *What is Art?*, we find Tolstoy still opposing the Greek discovery of the meaning of life in earthly happiness, beauty and strength to the Christian view that it lies in renunciation, humility and the love of others. This shows how deep and persistent was his sense of the contrast between the two views. There is certainly a strain in Tolstoy which sympathizes with his own Prince Andrew's hatred of the French and glories Homerically in the strength which threw them out, but there is also an equally powerful strain which sympathizes with the efforts of Princess Mary to turn her brother's thoughts away from revenge to Christian forgiveness. As R. F. Christian rightly says: 'To Tolstoy no war—not even a 'just' defensive war—can be anything but a human tragedy.' Homer, no doubt, could appreciate the tragedy of Hector, Andromache, Priam and the defeated Trojans; but even if Homer's work portrays many situations in which men must enact hell, he was basically reconciled to life on earth *as it is*. Nietzsche, indeed, thought that the fact that Homer made his gods so like men in their loves and hates was not only a kind of celebration of earthly life, but the best justification of it, and, in fact, the only true solution of the theodicy problem. The contrast between Tolstoy and Homer in this respect comes out in Tolstoy's protest *against* life on earth as it is, a protest which arises from his Christianity. Tolstoy would have seen the point of Ivan Karamazov's protest that, given the conditions of human life, he wants to 'return God his ticket'; and, indeed, Tolstoy himself furnished the great psychologist William James with an example of what James called 'the sick soul'. Tolstoy saw earthly life as in need of redemption and salvation, whereas Nietzsche condemned the very notion of such a need.

In considering where the truth in this momentous matter lies, it is necessary to begin by defining the theodicy problem more closely. The term 'theodicy' comes from two Greek words, *theos*, meaning god, and *diké*, meaning justice. The traditional theodicy problem was that of reconciling the belief in a divine justice of some kind with the indubitable existence of evil. The problem is presented in dramatic form in the *Prometheus* of Aeschylus and in the *Book of Job*. With the spread of monotheism and the development of the view that the one God's attributes include omnipotence and benevolence (which Homer's rival gods, of course, lack) the problem became even more acute, for it seems logically inconsistent to assume that God can be omnipotent and benevolent if evil exists.

—E. B. Greenwood, *Tolstoy: The Comprehensive Vision* (New York: St. Martin's Press, 1975): pp. 78–79.

# A. V. KNOWLES ON EARLY RUSSIAN CRITICISM

[A. V. Knowles was a lecturer in Russian at the University of Liverpool. Contemporary opinion quickly judges Tolstoy as "great," but early Russian critics were too embedded in their history to appreciate Tolstoy's epic view.]

⟨. . .⟩ Having failed to become a military leader of undying fame, Prince Andrey retires to his estates and grows depressed. Yet in this mood he does the only positive thing he ever manages in his whole life. He frees some three hundred of his serfs and transfers the rest from corvée to quit-rent. Does he though, asks Skabichevsky, do this out of respect for his fellow human beings? Does he do it as something that might restrain his arrogance, soften his hard heart or alleviate his vain melancholy? ⟨. . .⟩

Skabichevsky's final question epitomises the general tenor of much of the reaction of Tolstoy's contemporaries to *War and Peace* and to Prince Andrey in particular. While they certainly threw some light on him, both as a fictional character in his own right and as the mouthpiece of his creator, they mistook *War and Peace* for something it was not and consequently approached Prince Andrey from the wrong direction. They described him and what he did and suggested what he ought to have been and ought to have done. They discussed him primarily on the grounds of typicality and from widely held convictions on the role in the novel of a conventional fictional hero. They condemned him on moral grounds. They used him as a stick with which to beat Tolstoy and as a peg on which to hang their own ideas on literature, society, politics and history. They were as guilty of a subjective approach to him as they accused Tolstoy of being in his fiction. The reasons behind such opinions are many but include the following: *War and Peace* was published over a period of nearly five years and criticisms were printed on the appearance of each new instalment. It was markedly different both in conception and execution from what people had become accustomed to expecting a 'novel' to be. Tolstoy changed some of his ideas about it during its composition. His previous literary reputation had either been totally forgotten or only its negative side remembered. Perhaps another of the causes of the lack of a reasoned critical appraisal at the time had less to do with *War and Peace* itself than with the historical period of its appearance. The social and political atmosphere of the 1860s in Russia was of a particular kind. There was a feeling of release from the repressive reign of Nicholas I and it was a time of readjustment on a wide front following the revelations of the Crimean War. There was both hope for improvement in all walks of Russian life and despair at the growing realisation that nothing fundamental was actually happening. And it was a time of a widely felt desire for change but a hardening conviction that this would involve more than the form of 'edicts from above' and must include some tangible results for the mass of the population below. Such an atmosphere does not look conducive to the critical success or comprehension of a long and complicated work about Russian life and history some sixty years before. To many of its critics *War and Peace* had nothing to offer the society of the day except a largely unacceptable philosophy of conservatism and a mood of nostalgia. These might have been consoling to the upper classes with which the book was thought to be almost exclusively concerned, but writers should have something more to offer the country at large. Indeed most of the critics, typical for the period, tended to allow their comments to be guided entirely by their ideas on what role literature should play in society. Whatever their criteria, *War and Peace,* being what it is, was normally found wanting. It was not in fact until the 1880s that it began to receive some rather more positive critical appreciation.

—A. V. Knowles, *New Essays on Tolstoy,* ed. Malcolm Jones (Cambridge, England: Cambridge University Press, 1978): pp. 58–59.

## HENRY GIFFORD ON TOLSTOY'S VIEW OF ART

[Henry Gifford is an English critic who writes on Russian novelists. He edited the Maude translation of *War and Peace* (1983). Here he observes that Tolstoy's central belief that art was for communicating to "the people" links him with other writers, notably Wordsworth.]

What is popular, in the sense of being approved without further examination, held no interest at all for Tolstoy. His preoccupation was with something quite different, what is common to all who share in the trials of living, or what Rahv calls 'the most ordinary and therefore in their own way also the gravest occasions of life.' It could be said that Tolstoy restores the weight to such occasions. His hold on common experience was so strong that he could achieve simplicity without shallowness. It is not only in stories deliberately taking up the ideas and idiom of the people that Tolstoy shows himself a universal writer. Russian literature has nearly always been able to break through the limitations of class. Erich Auerbach noted this feature of Russian realism in *Mimesis*, concluding that it was 'based on a Christian and traditionally patriarchal concept of the creatural dignity of every human individual regardless of social rank and position . . .'. Tolstoy is intelligible at once to the simplest reader, and not only because he took such immense pains to make himself clear. It is even more a matter of feeling. He has an immediate effect, for he is always what Wordsworth held the poet to be, 'a man speaking to men.'

Tolstoy rejoiced in art because it gives

> the mysterious gladness of a communion which, reaching beyond the grave, unites with all men of the past who have been moved by the same feelings and with all men of the future who will yet be touched by them.

The idea had been expressed by Wordsworth in rather similar terms; and Joseph Conrad only a few years after Tolstoy, in 1897, was to speak of the 'conviction of solidarity' to which art responds. Conrad the exile felt to an unbearable degree the loneliness of the human condition; and Wordsworth, more confident of his membership in a simple community among the mountains, is yet at his most inspired moments a solitary. He speaks *for* the country people, but scarcely *with* them. Tolstoy, as individual and intransigent as ever man was, though he doubted so many things in his arduous search for meaning in life, felt the 'conviction of solidarity' so strongly that he always spoke to people of every condition. ⟨. . .⟩

The leading Russian poets of this century have all believed that they write for the people as a whole, who have need of them. ⟨. . .⟩

Th⟨e⟩ term, 'the people' has been often manipulated in political discourse, and nowhere more harmfully than in Russia. But the value is still there. Its Russian form, *narod*, has a peculiar resonance which cannot be conveyed in English. It implies the warmth of a family, who are children of the same motherland (*rodina*), and the cognate adjective, *rodnoy*, 'very own', expresses a heart-felt intimacy. Russian literature at its finest is conversation within the family, but the family is hospitable to all. The more truly national a writer in this sense, the more acceptable he becomes to the whole world; and that is the case with Tolstoy.

> —Henry Gifford, *Tolstoy* (Oxford: Oxford University Press, 1983): pp. 80–81.

## GARY SAUL MORSON ON REALISM AND PERSPECTIVE

[Gary Saul Morson teaches in the Department of Slavic Languages at Northwest University. He became president of the Tolstoy Society in 1991. In his study of *War and Peace* Morson observes that Tolstoy achieves realism through the absence of a dominant perspective.]

"*War and Peace* is what the author wished to express and was able to express in that form in which it is expressed," Tolstoy insisted, and might have added: "It was composed in the way in which the author composed it." Inventing a new kind of narrative, he attempted to invent a new penumbral genre of creation, conforming to the themes of the work and justifying its structure. ⟨. . .⟩

An author who follows this method, ⟨. . .⟩ does not know at the outset what the work will turn out to be when complete. Rather, beginning with only a loose set of principles and resources, the author allows the work to "shape itself" as it is being written. With no conclusion in mind, he deliberately cultivates the unexpected; structure is what it turns out to be, connections emerge without premeditation, and unity becomes only a unity of process. Integrity is ex post facto. ⟨. . .⟩

⟨I⟩n *War and Peace* it is not the narrator but the author, Leo Tolstoy himself, who claims not to know where the work is going, how long it will be, or what relationship, if any, will emerge to order its parts. ⟨. . .⟩ He surrenders this control deliberately, not because of some inspirational fit, but as a conscious method for constructing a particular kind of plot.

As we have seen, Tolstoy objected to the traditional plots of novels and histories, which he believed falsified the nature of reality, and, therefore, of the events they sought to describe. To summarize his objections: Incidents in these narratives derive meaning from their place within a generically given structure and in relation to an ending, but for Tolstoy such meanings are necessarily false. Foreshadowing, a source of narrative irony and aesthetic power, smuggles additional false meanings into events because, in Tolstoy's view, not just one but many possible futures may spring from any given moment. Each event figures in many possible sequences even though only one sequence is realized. Traditional narratives also falsify experience by relating only those events that fit their overall structure, whereas reality is composed of many moments that are radically irrelevant and have no significance whatsoever. Moreover, unlike novels and histories, life provides no privileged vantage point from which to judge characters and events. Pierre's unsuccessful search for an ideal place from which to view the battle at Borodino is emblematic of *War and Peace* as a whole. For Tolstoy, a criterion of true realism is the absence of privileged vantage points.

> —Gary Saul Morson, *Hidden in Plain View: Narrative and Creative Potentials in* War and Peace (Stanford, California: Stanford University Press, 1987): pp. 181–183.

RIMVYDAS SILBAJORIS ON THE HISTORICAL CONTEXT

[Rimvydas Silbajoris is a Lithuanian naturalized U. S. citizen who teaches Russian languages and literature at Ohio State University. *War and Peace* covers an important period of Russian and European history—much of which has been eclipsed for contemporary readers by the Cold War and current politics. In the introductory chapter to his study of Tolstoy Rimvydas Silbajoris provides a useful historical context for the reader.]

The most important ideological crosscurrents in nineteenth-century Russia belonged to the so-called Westernizers and Slavophiles. The westernizing movement had its roots in the seventeenth century, following ⟨. . .⟩ the invasion of Russia by Poland-Lithuania, during which many ideas and customs of the Catholic West spread throughout Russia. This influence was strengthened when, under the Empress Catherine II (1762–96), Russia gained the territories of the Ukraine and Byelorussia, both of which under the previous Polish rule had developed a number of Western-style cultural and social institutions. Catherine ⟨. . .⟩ tried to promulgate humanistic learning and liberal reforms in the governance of the empire. Some Russians became painfully aware that traditionally they had been different from Western Europe, that is, from the entire powerful growth of modern civilization initiated by the dawning of the New Age around 1492, and so they began to develop a Western-oriented mode of thought in the hope of bringing their country up to par with the West.

Tsar Peter I (1672–1725) undertook very vigorous and sweeping reforms, jolting the old Russia of the bojars (members of the landed gentry) into modern times, often with considerable violence. ⟨. . .⟩ In the eighteenth century, "Russia submitted with amazing wholeheartedness to the cultural values, myths, prejudices, and even objects emanating from France and elsewhere in Europe," and almost simultaneously its literature went through several Western movements that had taken some two or three centuries to develop, and that Russia had missed altogether, such as classicism, baroque, rococo, sentimentalism, and even romanticism.

After the Napoleonic Wars this orientation was much strengthened by some intellectuals cum officers in the Russian army who had marched into Paris in 1825 and seen the Western mode of life in Europe. Dreams of a constitutional monarchy and of the further westernization of Russia led to the failed Decembrist revolt, after which the traditional, conservative tsarist autocracy reasserted itself with crushing force. Pierre Bezukhov, the main hero of *War and Peace,* was originally conceived by Tolstoy as a Decembrist returned from exile. Thus the story of his ideological development includes the seminal force of all the Western ideas that sprung up in Russia before, during, and after the Napoleonic Wars. ⟨. . .⟩

Although attracted by the humanistic liberalism of the Westernizers, Tolstoy on the whole did not trust their mode of thought, just as he mistrusted and even opposed the entire edifice of Western civilization. In *War and Peace* we see this mistrust in the negative portrayals of Napoleon and other military leaders, whom Tolstoy shows as representing the Western penchant for rationalistic theorizing and model-building. We also see his anti-Westernism in Tolstoy's views of history, which he expressed throughout the novel in both expository argument and the portrayal of characters' destinies, as a pattern of random configurations of actions that stem from an impulse at the given moment; this view is in contrast to the logical causality in human affairs that served as the norm for a well-written novel in the West.

—Rimvydas Silbajoris, *War and Peace: Tolstoy's Mirror of the World* (New York: Twayne Publishers and Simon & Schuster Macmillan, 1995): pp. 4–6.

## NATASHA SANKOVITCH ON TOLSTOY'S USES OF REPETITION

[Natasha Sankovitch teaches in the Humanities and Classics Department at Ohio Wesleyan University. Repetition as a literary device is a signature feature of Tolstoy's writing. Some translators have eliminated repetions to make for what is assumed to be easier reading. In this extract Natasha Sankovitch discusses repetitiveness as a carefully considered conveyance for the writer's message.]

Repetition in Tolstoy's fictions is more than a mere stylistic device, for its use is fundamentally related to his understanding of human psychology and experience. Essentially, repetition for Tolstoy is the way the mind works: in perception the mind seizes on a detail that is familiar or striking, assigns a verbal form to the detail, which could be an object, an action, a concept, or a feeling, and reiterates this form as it brings the rest of experience—past, present, or anticipated—into focus around the key detail. This mental process is at work whether characters are trying to make sense of their experience, the narrator is trying to depict relationships among characters, the author is trying to establish certain themes, or readers are trying to shape multiple and various details into a coherent narrative.

For Tolstoy, repetition constitutes a principle or force of order imposed upon disorder. His characterizations suggest that he recognized the enormous psychological need for order and fear of chaos that makes human beings draw boundaries, make distinctions, repeat what is familiar. And it is not just order in immediate experience that is sought and valued, but also order over time: hence, we witness a complex and nearly indissoluble link between repetition and memory. Recurrences and meanings generated by recurrences are central to achieving a sense of continuity in history, the self, and in each text. Repetition in Tolstoy's fictions serves obvious narratological purposes: it contributes to characterization, plays a role in thematic and plot development, and can act as a mnemonic aid to readers, to list a few. But it is also fundamental to Tolstoy's exploration of philosophical questions, including how we acquire knowledge and how we ought to live. Repetition plays a critical role in his analysis of how human beings impose design on the seemingly endless continuum of their own and all physical nature. ⟨. . .⟩ Tolstoy takes advantage of the fact that repetition signals both sameness and difference, essence and relation, in order to depict perception and thought as mutually determining, continuous processes. ⟨. . .⟩

Tolstoy uses repetition to expose the conventions or codes of behavior that operate in group activity. Other times the repeated element sheds light on the relationships—the similarities and differences—between just two characters. In both cases, repetition also serves to define and illuminate particular themes or ideas in the book. By repeating the same thematic phrase in the quoted or narrated monologue of various characters in various contexts, Tolstoy depicts differing perspectives on the same issue. As readers sift through these perspectives, they acquire a kind of ethical education—an education in sympathy, understanding, and humility. Here especially repetition reflects Tolstoy's moral and sympathetic imagination: the depth and breadth of his conception of the complexities that constitute human experience and his ability to imagine and enter into positions other than his own. ⟨. . .⟩

⟨. . .⟩ Repetition becomes the means for the achievement of a sense of continuity and wholeness, a sense of harmony, without which the world seemed to Tolstoy hopelessly contingent, ephemeral, fragmented, and meaningless. For Tolstoy repetition is the key to how human beings create and recover experience.

—Natasha Sankovitch, *Recovering Experience: Repetition in Tolstoy* (Stanford, California: Stanford University Press, 1998): pp. 5–7, 10, 11.

# Plot Summary of
## *Anna Karenina*

*Anna Karenina* appears initially to be two parallel stories with separate and unrelated outcomes. The main characters—Anna and Levin—meet only once, and their stories (with a few changes in detail) could be unfolding in different regions and time periods in Russia with sufficient appeal to stand on their own. Tolstoy himself named the novel *Two Marriages* at an earlier point in its evolution. Elegant beautiful Anna has a natural place in upperclass Petersburg society with easy access to life's material wealth through her relationships with husband Karenin and lover Vronsky. Levin (even after marrying Kitty) is an awkward outsider in society and only at home in his beloved countryside where his wealth consists of family land which he must sustain with his own and his peasants' physical labor. Disorder, madness, and death end one story. Fruitful labor, life-giving insight, and a new generation end the other. A third story—Stiva and Dolly's marriage—does considerably overlap the other two (Stiva and Anna are siblings as are Dolly and Kitty), but their story could not stand alone.

Tolstoy was clear that a link existed between his stories. In a letter to his friend and critic N. N. Strakhov in April 1876, he wrote:

> . . . if the shortsighted critics think that I merely wanted to describe what appealed to me such as the sort of dinner Oblonsky has or what Anna's shoulders are like, then they are mistaken. In everything . . . I was guided by the need of collecting ideas, which, linked together would be the expression of myself. . . . it is impossible to express the sources of this interlinking directly in words; it can only be done indirectly by describing images, actions, and situations in words.

Although Tolstoy's words are sufficient it is likely that the reader in search of a link will suddenly remember that remarkable first sentence: "All happy families are like one another; each unhappy family is unhappy in its own way." This statement stands unconditionally outside the novel as if it arrived—if not straight from God then certainly as received wisdom for common readers like ourselves to ponder and reverently accept rather than dispute. Tolstoy said of writing *War and Peace* that he loved the national idea and in *Anna Karenina* the family idea. Recalling his long loyalty to finding the secret of human happiness inscribed on the green stick in his childhood it makes sense to conclude that Anna and Levin and all the other characters are linked in that larger dimension where all people, with differing levels of awareness, integrity, and fruitfulness, strive to make love work for happiness. In this realm we are all joined and Tolstoy's first sentence and epigraph have a didactic purpose.

Anna enters the reader's imagination before she enters the action of the novel. Summoned by Stiva in **Part I** to mend the domestic rupture caused by his infidelity, Anna is associated with harmony and her arrival with a heightened sense of life's dimensions. With Dolly and the children she is charming and at ease and speaks poignantly of Seryozha her son whom she has had to leave behind. By recalling Stiva's early love for Dolly and the virtuous consequences of forgiveness, Anna succeeds in persuading Dolly to be reconciled—restoring to one family the domestic stability she will soon destroy in her own. Levin enters the novel bashful and boyishly eager because he has come to Moscow to propose marriage to Kitty. He senses her presence before he sees her "by the joy and terror that gripped his heart." Kitty appreciates Levin but is currently infatuated by Vronsky who drops her to begin his single-focused pursuit of Anna whom he has met by chance at the railroad station. Levin returns despondently to his farm, grateful that his love for the land provides a genuine and consoling alternative. Stiva is restored to his customary cheerfulness, "careful not to let it show that, having been forgiven, he seemed to have forgotton his offense." Anna leaves Moscow fearing a dangerous attraction to Vronsky, but at a train stop discovers he has followed her with no intention of giving up. Anna and Vronsky witness a gruesome accidental death on the train track, an incident linking the novel's beginning and end.

In **Part II** Kitty visits a spa to heal her depression over Vronsky's rejection and meets Madame Stahl and Varenka. She makes a youthful mistake of admiring their professional "do-gooding" from which her discerning father rescues her, and offers innocent and genuine compassion to a dying man. After a year Anna's conscious resistance to Vronsky dissolves and they become lovers in a scene of seduction without sexual explicitness that permits Tolstoy to emphasize the lasting effect of the act. Anna learns the pleasures and anxieties of deception with Princess Betsy and friends. She includes Seryozha in some of her meetings with Vronsky to provide a semblance of innocence and later as an early effort to blend her separate lives, but these gestures damage her son who blames himself for something he knows is wrong and can't understand. Karenin, noticing other people's noticing of his wife's improprieties, makes a shaken but inadequate plea to return to the appearances of a proper marriage. A distracted Vronsky misrides his favorite horse in the steeplechase causing him to fall and her to die and Anna, watching with Karenin, to publicly display her passion for him. Levin meanwhile, still disconsolate, is enjoying his cows and the season of mowing.

**Part III** develops Levin's Tolstoy-like questioning and his engagement with the land. He wrestles with brother Sergey's challenging questions about working for the general good, and, despite his blissful experiences mowing with the peasants, decides to reorganize his farming methods to include a different role for peasant labor—a reform he judges essential for Russian agriculture. With difficulty Levin keeps at bay thoughts of Kitty. Karenin rejects the idea of a duel and proposes an arrangement that preserves Anna's relation to her son but forbids that with Vronsky, causing Anna to say ". . . oh God! Was ever a woman as unhappy as I am?" Vronsky, in contrast, has his code of rules for behavior as well as interests outside his life with Anna. Anna has no life beyond Vronksy. The inequality of their positions and differences in temperament create subtle dishonesties between them despite their passionate sexual union.

In **Part IV** Anna, Karenin, and Vronsky endure the awkwardness of their lives believing without evidence that some change will rescue them. Anna's decision to be free with Vronsky sets in motion events that entrap them both but Tolstoy simultaneously suggests that her passionate nature could not stay confined by life with Karenin. When Anna, near death after giving birth, summons Karenin to ask his forgiveness, all three make an effort to resolve an unendurable situation. Karenin rises to genuine forgiveness which moves and unbalances Anna and Vronsky. Anna welcomes death and Vronsky attempts suicide. The spiritual integrity required for such extreme measures is genuine but not sustainable. Anna lives, and, pining away without Vronksy, presents her desperate wish for death to Stiva, who, cheerfully believing "there's a way out of every situation," promises to arrange a divorce from Karenin. Karenin links divorce to Anna's separation from son so Anna refuses and flees to Italy with Vronsky. Levin meanwhile emerges from a despairing period by happily reconnecting with Kitty and feeling "as if he had grown a pair of wings."

Following his engagement to Kitty in **Part V** Levin enters a period of happy lunacy. Tolstoy presents the rapture of romantic love but also its dangerous capacity to fling its victims into extreme solipsism. Levin briefly (and humorously) believes all of life revolves around him. His effort to receive communion (required to be married in the church) without compromising his religious skepticism is fascinating and entertaining. Midpoint in the novel is their beautiful wedding. In Italy, Vronsky, still in love with Anna, experiences "the desire for desires—boredom." On a visit to the artist Mikhailov, Tolstoy's belief in the power of chance is dramatized when a drop of candle wax falling randomly on a discarded painting changes its entire configuration allowing the artist to bring it to life. A restless Anna and Vronsky return to Russia to live in the countryside while Levin discovers the ordinary annoyances of marriage, and he and Kitty work hard to understand one another and work together. When Levin leaves to attend his brother Nikolai's death, Kitty shows both independence and devotion by insisting on accompanying him. Watching Nikolai die plunges Levin into despairing questioning and Kitty into an energetic transformation of a dismal hotel room into a comforting and sanctified space. Their union generates a wholeness larger than each could produce alone. Lonely Karenin is befriended by the slippery Countess Lydia who persuades him to prevent Anna from seeing her son thus making inevitable Anna's desperate and daring and unbearably final visit to suffering Seryozha.

In **Part VI** Kitty and Levin create a fruitful and loving home capable of nourishing themselves and others. Levin enjoys the all-male adventures of hunting and continues to brood on his own character and other mysteries, but he and Kitty, especially once pregnant, are fully engaged in making new life. Kitty makes no special demands for herself while pregnant and during the beautiful jam-making scene is as solicitous of Agafya the peasant as she is of her visiting family. Anna's irrational jealousy intrudes on the apparently peaceful interludes she and Vronsky enjoy at his country estate and her happiness becomes increasingly precarious. She always postpones to "later" thinking about her impossible situation which has been grievously aggravated by society's rejection of her following a disastrous appearance at the opera.

Kitty and Levin's baby is born in the same chapter (**Part VII**) in which Anna dies. Still devoted, Vronsky comes up against his own limits and becomes exasperated with Anna's groundless and extreme jealousy and the irrational behavior it generates. A desperate visit to Dolly leaves Anna isolated in madness. An innocuous matter of timing produces a misunderstanding in the midst of their estrangement causing Anna and Vronsky to lose each other forever.

**Part VIII** was published separately and criticized by some for its treatment of the Russian volunteer effort to defend the oppressed Slavs in Turkey. The reader learns that Karenin assumes care for both children; Vronsky, permanently destroyed by loss of Anna and his lineage, heads for the war. Kitty grows spiritually with motherhood and Levin comes upon a resolution of his questioning by discovering with the help of peasant wisdom that life's truth comes not through the intellect but with the gift of living.

Readers respond differently to Anna's fate. Tolstoy raises the question of moral responsibility; the human capacity to choose, understand, and suffer; and the passionate quality of life that expresses itself in each individual life. In his choice of the Biblical passage about the Lord's vengeance, Tolstoy invokes a sense of an implacable human nature given by God with inevitable consequences following acts of human frailty, but in the novel itself he makes the reader mindful of the importance of forgiving and, implicitly, that other commandment: Judge not. ✤

# List of Characters in
## *Anna Karenina*

**Anna Karenina:** A strikingly beautiful woman with a mass of black hair and statuesque carriage—possesses a natural vitality and will too passionate to find expression in her world. She marries a man particularly ill-suited to her but she chooses a lover, who, although compelling and attractive, has conspicuously less dimension and depth than she does. Ironically appearing in the novel first as a successful family peacemaker, Anna lives perilously close to an edge carrying the irreconcilable loves for Vronsky and her son and an unceasing need to be at home somewhere.

**Konstantin Dimitryvich Levin**—"never bored in his own company"—carries important ideological themes for Tolstoy. He is identified with the fertile ancestral land of the Tsarist reign in Russia, and, desiring to be a responsible nobleman, focuses on economic problems, agriculture, and the prosperity of the peasants following the Emancipation. Never comfortable in the city, Levin experiences a blissful oneness with life uncomplicated by strategy, status, or possessiveness. Nikolai's death stirs deep dread in Levin and anguished questioning which is of no practical use to his dying brother. His marriage to Kitty, who both upstages and complements him at Nikolai's death, provides thematic contrasts to those of Dolly and Stiva, Anna and Vronsky, and Anna and Karenin.

**Kitty Shcherbatskya** successfully emerges from society with the attendant amorous attentions of many young men to become an animated beautiful woman capable of an unmediated response to life and the compassionate devotion of a mature faith. Rejected by Vronsky, her honesty won't permit her to be comforted by "hypocritical expressions of sympathy" and she falls into a depression misdiagnosed as physical illness. At a spa to restore her health, Tolstoy says she possesses "the suppressed fire of life." She displays a readiness for kindness and mercy for which she will find a proper context. Kitty is fully a match for Levin.

"Every moment of [**Alexei Karenin's**] life," according to Tolstoy, "was filled up and carefully apportioned." Husband of Anna for nine years, he is mainly preoccupied with the bureaucratic functioning of his high-level but dull government post. His discovery of Anna's unfaithfulness causes genuine pain but his main response is to restore normal marital appearances while ensuring that Anna suffers the deprivation of her lover. Despite an absence of generous vitality, Karenin can sustain brief moments of compassion, and, when he thinks Anna is dying giving birth to a child not his own, makes remarkably poignant gestures of forgiveness, which, however, he is unable to sustain. Karenin makes an effort to relate to his forlorn son but fails to recognize the boy's lonely and perplexed suffering.

**Count Alexei Vronsky** is an intelligent and debonair nobleman with an aspiring military career. His sudden passion for Anna awakens her immense vitality, which, once released, he is unable to fully match or understand. He makes clear (when spurning Kitty) that he has no interest in family life and thus serves as contrast to both Levin and Stiva. Vronsky lives by a code of rules that defines his behavior for all contingencies except the ones created by his love for Anna. A quality of reckless destructiveness causes his favorite horse to fall and break her back.

**Stiva Oblonsky** is Dolly's high-spirited, easy-going, unfaithful husband who adores but neglects their children. Not genuinely remorseful about his infidelity, but genuinely concerned about preserving the sanctity of his family, Stiva summons Anna his sister as a peacemaker. Reproached by Levin for a later tryst Stiva responds characteristically with his cheerful pragmatism: no harm will come to his wife, much pleasure is to be had for him, so there is no problem. Stiva's energzy and generosity lighten the novel but we like him less as we watch his indulgences bring deprivation to his family. Stiva's ingratiating charm over others is likened to the effect of almond oil.

**Dolly** is a completely maternal presence in the novel. Her love for Stiva—with Anna's encouragement—eclipses her painful humiliation over her husband's infidelity. Dolly appears overwhelmed by duties to home and children but she is partly rescued by them as well. Anxious questions about life's purpose do not disturb Dolly. As sister to Kitty, Dolly plays a role in bringing about her marriage to Levin. Her sudden departure from Anna and Vronsky's home hastens Anna's descent into isolation and madness.

**Nikolai Levin,** Levin's half brother, lives in poverty with a former prostitute. He holds onto a hope of building a Socialist workers' guild, which his illness will prevent from happening. Nikolai's death brings Levin to deeper questioning and self-awareness and evokes Kitty's practical and compassionate generosity.

**Sergey Koznyshev** "known to all of Russia" for his intellectual writings, appears initially to overshadow his half brother Levin but lacks, according to Levin, "the weakness necessary [to love]. . ." as well as Levin's own vitality and connectedness. He fails to propose to Varenka; he sleeps while Levin mows; and, claiming to love nature, ruins a meadow rushing over it to a fishing stream.

**Princess Betsy Tverskaya** is the guardian of Petersburg society's cleverly crafted morals. She enjoys golf and the successful management of social scandals. Cousin to Vronsky and a relation by marriage to Anna, she easily enables their illicit relationship. Princess Betsy's elegant drawing rooms are the site for Anna's first pleasure and anxiety of losing one's integrity in society.

**Countess Lydia Ivanovna** who "had never ceased to be in love with someone," turns with multiple motives to Karenin after Anna leaves: an interest in companionship; a wish to hurt Anna; and the pleasure of scandal. Lydia tells Seryozha that Anna is dead and persuades Karenin to block the reunion of Anna and her son.

**Countess Vronskaya** is Vronsky's widowed mother; an aging, amoral society belle who initiates Anna's interest in her son then joins society's condemnation that contributes to Anna's death.

**Madame Stahl** an invalid upperclass woman, and **Mademoiselle Varenka,** her unpaid younger helper, "who had never been youthful"—both Russians—are do-gooders whose formal religious piety attracts an innocent when their lives overlap at the restorative spa in Germany. Varenka befriends Kitty and nearly achieves a desirable marriage through the friendship.

**Seryozha,** youngest son of Anna and Karenin, is loved by his mother as much as she loves her lover and when he is not chosen by her, he becomes the first victim of her fate. In the presence of his distant father, Seryozha feels himself to be an "imaginary boy." ❀

# Critical Views on
## *Anna Karenina*

DOSTOEVSKY ON *ANNA KARENINA* AS A DISTINCTLY
RUSSIAN NOVEL

[F. M. Dostoevsky, Russian writer and contemporary of Tolstoy best known for his profound insights about human
behavior, greatly influenced the 20th century novel. His
books include *Crime and Punishment* (1866) and *The
Brothers Karamazov* (1880). In his review of *Anna Karenina,*
Dostoevsky clarifies the differences between the European
and Russian world views especially as related to evil and
human frailty. He praises the novel as an embodiment of
Russian wisdom but laments that Tolstoy appears to desert
these views in the separately published eighth chapter.]

*Anna Karenina* is perfection as a work of art, and a work that turned
up just at the right time, and also one with which none of the European literatures of the present epoch can compare. Moreover,
according to its main idea it is a peculiarly Russian, indigenous
piece, representing that which constitutes the difference between us,
Russians, and the European world. ⟨. . .⟩ In *Anna Karenina* a certain
view of human guilt and criminality is expressed. Human beings are
depicted in abnormal circumstances. Evil existed before them.
Caught in a whirlpool of falsehoods, they transgress and perish
inevitably: obviously an idea that has been near and dear to European thinkers for a long time. How, then, is this problem solved in
Europe? All over Europe it is handled in a twofold manner. One
solution is as follows: the law has been laid down, framed, formulated, developed and refined for thousands of years. Evil and good
are defined, weighed, their measurements are taken and degrees
defined historically by the sages of mankind in tireless efforts to
fathom the human soul as well as by precise scientific research into
the extent of the unifying power of communal living. This elaborate
code must be obeyed blindly. ⟨. . .⟩ "I know," says their civilization,
"that this is all very blind and inhuman and really impossible,
because one cannot work out the final formula for the human
problem while mankind is still only halfway down the road of its
evolution; nevertheless since there is no other way, one must stick to

that which is written and stick to it verbatim and without humanitarian considerations. ⟨. . .⟩" The other solution is the opposite: "Since society is still organized abnormally, individuals cannot be called to account for its abuses and consequences. Therefore a criminal is not responsible for his actions, and for the time being there can be no such thing as a crime. In order to do away with crimes and human guilt, the abnormal nature of society and its structure must first be dealt with. Since to cure the existing order of things would take a long time and would be hopeless anyway, and besides there are no cures, one must destroy the entire society and sweep away the old order as if with a broom. ⟨. . .⟩"

In the Russian author's approach to human delinquency ⟨. . .⟩ no elimination of poverty, and no organization of fair labor practices will save mankind from abnormality and, consequently, from guilt and criminality. This vastly complex idea is executed with formidable psychological analysis of the human soul, reaching enormous depth and power of artistic portrayal and unparalleled realism. What is made clear and plausible to the point of obviousness is that evil is rooted in mankind deeper than any socialists, clumsy healers of social ills, will concede; that no form of social organization can dispose of evil; that the human soul is what it is, that abnormality and sin issue from its own fiber, and, finally, that the laws of human consciousness are as yet so utterly unknown, so totally unexplored by science, so undefined, and so mysterious that, for the time being at least, there are not, and cannot be, any healers or *final* judges of human problems other than He who says "Vengeance is mine; I shall repay."

—F. M. Dostoevsky, *Diary of a Writer* (Paris: YMCA Press, 1877): pp. 278–286. Trans. by Boris Sorokin, *Critical Essays on Tolstoy*, ed. Edward Wasiolek (Boston: G. K. Hall & Co., 1986): pp. 127–128.

## ANONYMOUS ON THE MORAL LESSONS

Count Tolstoi's *Anna Karénina* is a long, intricate, and crowded novel of Russian life. It is really two novels, we might almost say three novels, in one. It sets out with an unhappy domestic experience, in which Prince Stepan Oblonsky is detected by his wife, Darya, in a *liaison* with the French governess of their children, the husband barely escaping an irretrievable rupture with her whom he has wronged. But this is only an introduction—a dish of soup before meat. From this beginning the story branches in two lines: one following the innocent but tearful experiences of Konstantin Levin and Kitty Shcherbatskaïa, together with the fortunes of Levin as a large landed proprietor in connection with agrarian problems of a socialistic kind; the other the guilty love of Count Alekséi Vronsky for Anna Karénina, the wife of Alekséi Karénin, their defiant and illicit union, and the tragic fate which concludes their history. This variety of interests and motives, the multiplicity of characters, and a confusion as to names which the translator might have saved his readers by a stern independence of Russian nomenclature, make the opening chapters perplexing and toilsome; until the stream of the story gets fairly under way and falls clearly into its several channels. ⟨. . .⟩

The two leading themes act as if one were set as a foil to the other; Vronsky's and Anna's lawless passion and its fruits over against Levin's agrarian experiments on his country estate of Pokrovsky. The great mass of materials employed gives cumbersomeness and complexity to the product, molded though it be by a powerful and steady hand. The reader does not ever feel that the guide is losing the way, but rather that he is being led through a mountainous and rugged country, with an immense range of ground to cover, and ground of a difficult character. ⟨. . .⟩

As a socialistic novel *Anna Karénina* is wholesome, and for a novel on the transgression of the Seventh Commandment it is inoffensive. Yet on its latter side, on these relations of the sexes, on the facts of parentage and motherhood, the book speaks with a plainness of meaning, sometimes with a plainness of words, which is at least new. We do not know that we have ever before read a novel in which the details of an *accouchement*, for example, were made to do service for one chapter. A very effective chapter it is of its kind, but—!

With the moral intent of the work no fault can be found. The sinfulness of sin, the wretchedness of sin, the bitter fruits of sin, are all in the sad story of Vronsky and Anna. ⟨. . .⟩

The great lesson of Anna Karénina's melancholy history is that for a woman to marry a man twenty years her senior when she does not love him, is to place her under conditions of terrible temptation when afterwards she comes to be thrown with a man whom she can love, and who is not unselfish enough to save her from herself when she has put herself in his power; and that, surrendering to that temptation, the wages of her sin is—death.

It must have taken some resolution to translate this book, and some courage to publish it; and the reading of it some persons will find a work which requires perseverance and application. But it is large and strong; we remember nothing with which exactly to compare it since Elizabeth De Ville's *Johannes Olaf* of 1873.

—Anonymous on the Moral Lessons of *Anna Karenina*. Trans. Nathan Haskell Dole for *Literary World* 17 (April 1886), *Critical Essays on Tolstoy*, ed. Edward Wasiolek (Boston: G. K. Hall & Co., 1986): pp. 121–122.

## MATTHEW ARNOLD ON THE DIFFERENCES BETWEEN *ANNA KARENINA* AND *MADAME BOVARY*

[Matthew Arnold, English poet and critic, was known as the "apostle of culture." He is best remembered for his poem "Dover Beach" and his essays *Culture and Anarchy* (1869). Arnold notes that both are novels of passion but important differences are reflected in Anna's manner of death.]

We have been in a world which misconducts itself nearly as much as the world of a French novel all palpitating with "modernity." But there are two things in which the Russian novel—Count Tolstoi's novel at any rate—is very advantageously distinguished from the type of novel now so much in request in France. In the first place, there is no fine sentiment, at once tiresome and false. We are not told to believe, for example, that Anna is wonderfully exalted and ennobled by her passion for Wronsky. The English reader is thus saved from many a groan of impatience. The other thing is yet more important. Our Russian novelist deals abundantly with criminal passion and with adultery, but he does not seem to feel himself owing any service to the goddess Lubricity, or bound to put in touches at this goddess's dictation. Much in *Anna Karénine* is painful, much is unpleasant, but nothing is of a nature to trouble the senses, or to please those who wish their senses troubled. This taint is wholly absent. In the French novels where it is so abundantly present its baneful effects do not end with itself. Burns long ago remarked with deep truth that it *petrifies feeling*. Let us revert for a moment to the powerful novel of which I spoke at the outset, *Madame Bovary*. Undoubtedly the taint in question is present in *Madame Bovary*, although to a much less degree than in more recent French novels, which will be in every one's mind. But *Madame Bovary*, with this taint, is a work of *petrified feeling*; over it hangs an atmosphere of bitterness, irony, impotence; not a personage in the book to rejoice or console us; the springs of freshness and feeling are not there to create such personages. Emma Bovary follows a course in some respects like that of Anna, but where, in Emma Bovary is Anna's charm? The treasures of compassion, tenderness, insight, which alone, amid such guilt and misery, can enable charm to subsist and to emerge, are wanting to Flaubert. He is cruel, with the cruelty of petrified feeling, to his poor heroine; he pursues her without pity or pause, as with malignity; he is harder upon her himself than any reader even, I think, will be inclined to be.

—Matthew Arnold, *Essays in Criticism* (New York: Macmillan, 1888). *Critical Essays on Tolstoy*, ed. Edward Wasiolek (Boston: G. K. Hall & Co., 1986): p. 141.

## DERRICK LEON ON LEVIN AS TOLSTOY

[Tolstoy's characters often embody some aspect of his own far-ranging interests. Derrick Leon notes in his biographical study of Tolstoy the multiple passions for land and family that link the writer with Levin.]

It is in the study of Levin that we are able to trace the evolution of Tolstoy's personal emotional experience, from the moment of the terrible, blank sense of negation which began to obsess him at the time he had finished *War and Peace,* until the time when, nearly ten years later, he had completed *A Confession.* ⟨. . .⟩

At ⟨Levin's⟩ brother's death (which is a re-created episode based partly upon the death of Dmitri and partly upon the death of Nicholas, to suit the needs of his story) Levin seriously, and for the first time, considers man's mortality. "Death, the inevitable end of everything, confronted him for the first time with irresistible force. . . . It was within himself too, he felt it. If not to-day, then to-morrow, or thirty years hence, was it not all the same? But what that inevitable death was, he not only did not know, not only had never considered, but could not and dared not consider. ⟨...⟩"

Once this realization had been established in him with sufficient depth, there was no evading it. "The paths of glory lead but to the grave" was no longer a skilful poetic phrase, but a grim reality. Despite his material well-being and his immense capacity for enjoyment; his loved and loving wife; the satisfaction of exercising his powerful, healthy body mowing with the peasants; the instinctive, almost physical communion with nature he feels when hunting and shooting, this idea continues to haunt him with an increasing frequency and an urgency that will not be denied. "⟨...⟩ And so one passes one's life finding distraction in hunting or in work, merely not to think of death!"

The inner truth of such a state of mind is a fact known to all genuine psychologists. Pascal expressed it perfectly when he wrote: "Nothing is so insufferable to man as to be completely at rest, without passions, without business, without diversion, without study. He then feels his nothingness, his forlornness, his insufficiency, his dependence, his weakness, his emptiness. There will immediately arise from the depths of his heart weariness, gloom, sadness, fretfulness, vexation, despair." But Levin soon reaches a further stage when all distractions cease to have effect, and the condition that arises during their absence persists in spite of them. Unlike Prince Andrew, whose problems are solved by death, and Pierre, who finds a temporary solution in the satisfactions of married life, Levin is fully aware that the only true solution must be wrested from himself, by some fusion of understanding in his warring intelligence and emotions. ⟨...⟩ For him the problem was this: 'If I don't accept the replies offered by Christianity to the questions my life presents, what solutions do I accept?' . . . He was in the position of a man seeking food in a toyshop or at a gunsmith's. . . . 'Without knowing what I am, and why I am here, it is impossible to live. Yet I cannot know that, and therefore I cannot live.' . . . And though he was a happy and healthy family man, Levin was several times so near to suicide that he hid a cord he had lest he should hang himself, and feared to carry a gun lest he should shoot himself."

—Derrick Leon, *Tolstoy: His Life and Work* (London: Routledge, 1944): pp. 175–177.

## JAMES T. FARRELL ON THE COLLISION OF VALUES IN RUSSIAN SOCIETY

[James T. Farrell was a prolific American author in the naturalist tradition best known for his novel *Studs Lonigan* (1935). Farrell points out that *Anna Karenina* was written during a period of Russian history full of exciting contradictions. Questions were raised that required highly personal—as opposed to societal—answers. Farrell discusses Anna's life as emblematic of the period.]

Among the works of nineteenth-century Russian literature, *Anna Karenina* is focal. No other Russian novel of the entire century so concentrates the so-called Russian problem, images and represents it so vividly, so directly, so immediately in terms of direct, vigorously drawn, and humanly credible characterizations. The fact that it is set in the time of most intense change in Russia is significant in understanding the novel. The intensity of the change, the transitional character of the times, the fact that Levin, the most intelligent character in *Anna Karenina*, realizes that everything is upside down and just taking shape—all this helps us to understand the richness, the all-sidedness, the significance of this work.

⟨. . .⟩ Anna is the most representative figure in this novel. She is symbolic. She is Tolstoy's image of humanity. ⟨. . .⟩ Her motivations come from inside herself, and are not seriously influenced by her role, her function in society. She acts in accordance with her inner nature, and she wants, above all else, to love and to be loved. We know from Tolstoy's entire literary output that he considered the need to love and to be loved fundamental in the character of the natural man and woman. Anna is, then, the most natural member of the upper classes to be found in this work. Her actions are inspired by her emotions. ⟨. . .⟩ Love, not social convenience, not social ritual, not social codes of morals, honor, and prestige, is Anna's guide. Her tragedy is that of humanity seeking to express the full nature of its need to love and to be loved in material, sensory, sexual relationships; and this, it should be added, is sought amid a setting of luxury.

⟨. . .⟩ The central problem treated is thus that of freedom, freedom and the self, or the personality. It is this same problem which concerns us at the present moment, in a further advanced period of our historical development; in fact, we can say we face this problem from the other side of progress. ⟨...⟩

When Anna and Vronsky are living on his estate in their last happy period, they have everything that is new and most luxurious. They are living on the scale of the advanced West. And in their conversation they speak of America and the American Way. It was Tolstoy's conclusion, in the first stages of Western progress in Russia, that this Way was not capable of feeding the deepest needs of humanity. *Anna Karenina* establishes his view in terms of the living images of human beings. Tolstoy's alternative, the so-called doctrine of Tolstoyism based on non-resistance and individual moral self-regeneration, has not, however, been historically successful. When we read him, then, we must do so not for some rigid solution but for insight. *Anna Karenina* brings us face to face with a great mind, a great artist, and a work of artistic greatness which is one of the true masterpieces of world literature.

> —James T. Farrell, *Literature and Morality* (New York: Vanguard Press, Inc., 1945): pp. 298–299, 303–304.

## R. P. BLACKMUR ON CONFRONTING THE IMMEDIACY OF EXPERIENCE IN *ANNA KARENINA*

[R. P. Blackmur, associated with the "New Criticism" in literature, was professor of English at Princeton. He was widely admired as literary and social critic; his *The Lion and the Honeycomb* was published in 1955. The turbulence of Russian society led some to complacency and others to anguish. Blackmur notes the consequences that follow different responses.]

If there is one notion which represents what Tolstoy is up to in his novels—emphatically in *Anna Karenina* and *War and Peace*—it is this: He exposes his created men and women to the "terrible ambiguity of an immediate experience" (Jung's phrase in his *Psychology and Religion*), and then, by the mimetic power of his imagination, expresses their reactions and responses to that experience. Some reactions are merely protective and make false responses; some reactions are so deep as to amount to a change in the phase of being and make honest responses. The reactions are mechanical or instinctive, the responses personal or spiritual. But both the reactions and the responses have to do with that force greater than ourselves, outside ourselves, and working on ourselves, which whether we call it God or Nature is the force of life, what is shaped or misshaped, construed or misconstrued, in the process of living. ⟨. . .⟩

⟨. . .⟩ Stiva and Dolly are too near the actual manner of things, are too wholly undifferentiated from the course of society and of individuals, ever to feel the need or the pang of rebirth. All they want is for things to be as they are. ⟨. . .⟩ Anna craves to transmute what moves her from underneath—*all* that can be meant by libido, not sex alone—into personal, individual, independent love; she will be stronger than society because she is the strength of society, but only so in her death at the hands of society. Levin craves to transmute himself upwards, through society, into an individual example of the love of God; he, too, will be stronger than society because he finds the will of God enacted in the natural order of things of which society is a part, but he will only do so as long as God is with him in his life. What separates both Anna and Levin from the ruck of rebels is that they make their rebellions, and construct their idylls, through a direct confrontation and apprehension of immediate experience. There is nothing arbitrary about their intentions, only their decisions; there is nothing exclusive or obsessed about their perceptions, only their actions. They think and know in the same world as Stiva and Dolly, and indeed they had to or they could never have been in love with such eminently natural creatures as Vronsky and Kitty. They live in the going concern of society, and they are aside from it only to represent it the better.

—R. P. Blackmur, *Eleven Essays in the European Novel* (New York: Harcourt, Brace & World, Inc., 1964), reprinted in *Tolstoy: A Collection of Critical Essays*, ed. Matlaw, (Englewood Cliffs, New Jersey: Prentice Hall, Inc., 1967): pp. 127–129.

# LIONEL TRILLING ON TOLSTOI'S AFFECTION FOR HIS CHARACTERS

[Lionel Trilling, American literary and cultural critic, taught at Columbia. He wrote *The Liberal Imagination* (1950) and *Sincerity and Authenticity* (1972). In this extract from *The Opposing Self* (1955) Trilling compares the realism in Tolstoy's writing with that of Homer and links this quality to a profound benevolence both writers felt toward their characters.]

This quality of lifelikeness, which, among all novelists, he possesses to the highest degree, does not make Tolstoi the greatest of novelists. ⟨. . .⟩ he can be called the most *central* of novelists. It is he who gives to the novel its norm and standard, the norm and standard not of art but of reality. ⟨. . .⟩

Only one other writer has ever seemed to his readers to have this normative quality—what we today are likely to feel about Tolstoi was felt during the eighteenth century in a more positive and formulated way about Homer. ⟨. . .⟩

One of the ways of accounting for the normative quality of Homer is to speak of his objectivity. Homer gives us, we are told, the object itself without interposing his personality between it and us. He gives us the person or thing or event without judging it, as Nature itself gives it to us. And to the extent that this is true of Homer, it is true of Tolstoi. But again we are dealing with a manner of speaking. Homer and Nature are of course not the same, and Tolstoi and Nature are not the same. Indeed, what is called the objectivity of Homer or of Tolstoi is not objectivity at all. Quite to the contrary, it is the most lavish and prodigal subjectivity possible, for every object in the *Iliad* or in *Anna Karenina* exists in the medium of what we must call the author's love. But this love is so pervasive, it is so constant, and it is so equitable, that it creates the illusion of objectivity, for everything in the narrative, without exception, exists in it as everything in Nature, without exception, exists in time, space, and atmosphere. ⟨. . .⟩ For Tolstoi everyone and everything has saving grace. Like Homer, he scarcely permits us to choose between antagonists—just as we dare not give all our sympathy either to Hector or to Achilles, nor, in their great scene, either to Achilles or to Priam, so we cannot say, as between Anna and Alexei Karenin, or between Anna and Vronsky, who is right and who is wrong.

⟨. . .⟩ It is when the novelist really loves his characters that he can show them in their completeness and contradiction, in their failures as well as in their great moments, in their triviality as well as in their charm. ⟨. . .⟩

It is a subtle triumph of Tolstoi's art that it induces us to lend ourselves with enthusiasm to its representation of the way things are. We so happily give our assent to what Tolstoi shows us and so willingly call it reality because we have something to gain from its being reality. For it is the hope of every decent, reasonably honest person to be judged under the aspect of Tolstoi's representation of human nature. Perhaps, indeed, what Tolstoi has done is to constitute as reality the judgment which every decent, reasonably honest person is likely to make of himself—as someone not wholly good and not wholly bad, not heroic yet not without heroism, not splendid yet not without moments of light, not to be comprehended by any formula yet having his principle of being, and managing somehow, and despite conventional notions, to maintain an unexpected dignity.

—Lionel Trilling, *The Opposing Self* (New York: Viking, 1955): pp. 66–75.

## Renato Poggioli on Anna's Seduction

[Renato Poggioi was professor of Slavic and Comparative Literature at Harvard. In this extract from *The Spirit of the Letter* Poggioli discusses Tolstoy's restraint in describing the seduction scene when he used such elaborate realistic detail for other human activities.]

The foundations of *Anna Karenina* are grounded on the opposition of the ethos of family life and the pathos of unlawful love. Thus the structure of the second of Tolstoy's great novels is very similar to that of the first. Even here the fundamental opposition merges with parallel and lesser contrasts, such as those between "town" and "country," the new and the old capital, the frivolities of 'high life' and the labors of the fields. Here we have, however, a novel of modern life, without hopes for a better future or longings after a better past. The reader is confronted with two dramas, the one public, the other private. Socially *Anna Karenina* is a "tragedy of manners," or, as Dostoevsky would say, a "drawing-room tragedy." But morally it is another version of what the old Tolstoy, in a conversation reported by Gorky, was to call the worst of all tragedies: the "tragedy of the bedroom." But it was chiefly in the discreet treatment, and indirect representation, of the latter that Tolstoy again showed that his talent consisted in a unique fusion of literary intelligence and ethical insight.

It is evident that Tolstoy projected Anna's drama through a double perspective, based on the sublime absurdity of the Christian injunction to love the sinner and to hate his sin. He wanted the reader to be merciful, not merciless as was society, which punished Anna not for sinning but for confessing her passion before the world; yet he wanted him to be severe, as well as merciful. Anna was to be pitied but not absolved, nor was her guilt to be forgiven. Tolstoy realized, however, that in order to determine such an ideal moral balance he had to pass over in silence the fatal moment when Anna yields once and for ever to the seduction of sin. For a psychologist like Tolstoy, who looked with clear eyes at the 'facts of life', and who later dared to tear all veils from the realities of sexual love, this was not an easy thing to do. Yet, had he done otherwise, he would have hardly escaped one or the other of two pitfalls: on one hand the naturalistic portrayal, on the other the romantic idealization, of the sexual act. Tolstoy knew that Anna Karenina could not undergo the self-inflicted indignities of an Emma Bovary. He also knew that she could be neither a Francesca nor an Iseult: that neither she nor her creator could speak aloud of her sin. This is why, with great intellectual courage, he made an act of renunciation, motivated not by puritan scruples but by an artist's concern. In brief, he resisted the temptation of describing Anna's fall. Anna's fall takes place outside the novel, behind closed doors: and the author reports it, anticlimactically, as a *fait accompli*. We are informed of what has just occurred by a series of suspension dots, which open a chapter dealing only with what happens immediately afterwards.

—Renato Poggioli, *The Spirit of the Letter* (Cambridge: Harvard University Press, 1965).

[The question of Anna's fate—tragic or pathetic, deserving
of compassion or contempt—continues with each generation of readers. In this extract from *Introduction to Tolstoy's
Writings* Simmons presents one prominent view.]

Anna's tragedy unfolds slowly, naturally, remorselessly, before a large
audience of the social worlds of two capitals, of the countryside, and
elsewhere. But nearly all the fully realized characters, including the
brilliantly portrayed Oblonsky and Shcherbatsky families, are
involved in one way or another with the fate of these two star-
crossed lovers. For Tolstoy, himself a bit in love with his heroine's
large, generous, radiant nature, endeavors to show that she is as
much a victim of the hypocrisy of this high society as of her own
passion. If Anna had had an affair with a handsome, socially desirable army officer, high society would not have condemned her provided she was discreet and abided by conventions that were
supposed to make such affairs permissible. The only one hurt would
have been her husband, but this was the generally accepted order of
things. Above all, appearances must be kept up. Vronsky's mother
thought it entirely *comme il faut* that her son should have a liaison
with a charming woman such as Anna; it added a degree of social
polish to a rising young careerist. So are Stiva Oblonsky's easy adul-
teries accepted by his society; only in the case of his wife do they
cause a bit of pain, but not disaster.

Anna, however, is no casual adulteress. Her love for Vronsky is a
deep and lasting passion for which she is prepared to flout conven-
tion, sacrifice her security, leave her husband's home, and compromise him openly. She places herself beyond the pale of her social
class, but only because of the manner in which she transgresses its
hypocritical moral code. Her real suffering begins, not when she
deserts her husband, but when she receives the snubs of her
friends. In a happy mood just before the birth of his child, Levin is
moved to visit Anna. She receives him with the gracious manner of
a woman of good society, self-possessed and natural. He immediately becomes at ease and comfortable as though he had known
her from childhood. But after he returns home he suffers a revulsion of feeling and, encouraged by Kitty, he thinks of Anna again as
a fallen woman. She is the outsider, shut off from the self-confident

life of the family. Indeed, the contrast between the marriage of Levin and Kitty, which moves ever outward to include more and more of society, and the affair of Vronsky and Anna, which leaves Anna in her carriage looking out on a city that has finally exiled her socially, only serves to intensify our sympathy for her plight. It is a measure of the moral balance Tolstoy preserves in his portrayal of Anna that he persuades his readers to judge her severely, but with compassion.

—Ernest J. Simmons, *Introduction to Tolstoy's Writings* (Chicago: University of Chicago Press, 1968): pp. 86–87.

## ELIZABETH GUNN ON *ANNA KARENINA* AS ADULT FICTION

[Elizabeth Gunn, an English novelist, also wrote a biography of Dorothy Wordsworth, and here offers some observations about family happiness in the novel.]

⟨. . .⟩ Oblonsky, the roué, is the only happy person in the book. And how, we may ask, does he contrive to achieve happiness? 'The answer is . . . live from day to day; in other words forget, but as he could not find forgetfulness in sleep, at least not until bedtime, nor return to the music sung by the little decanter women, he must therefore lose himself in the dream of life.'

To this extent, no more, Stepan Arkadyevitch may be said to prepare the way for Anna. But no, there is one other sentence. He is thinking of his unfaithfulness, of Dolly. '"No she will never forgive me—she cannot forgive me. And the worst of it is that I am to blame for everything—I am to blame and yet I am not to blame. That is the whole tragedy," he mused.'

This is an adult tragedy, by which I do not mean that Stepan Arkadyevitch is himself adult; but merely that when we are adult there is no one else to blame. We are both to blame and not to blame. We are what we have unconsciously, unthinkingly become. Not only are we not in control—we are no longer, as youth assumes, allowed the illusion of being so. The very qualities which go to make the enjoyment of Stepan Arkadyevitch are the identical qualities which create Anna's suffering.

The very buoyancy which has enabled Anna to survive her marriage to Karenin has allowed her to come through life too easily, without a struggle, without developing strength of character. She has lacked the compulsive streak which forges such a strength. She is, without being aware of it, rudderless. Moreover, all her life she has lacked passionate love. She has never been adored by her parents. She had none. Is this her fault? What woman in a similar position would not be conquered by such love, tenderness, passion, as Vronsky's?

If we stand back and pause with Matvey, his valet, to admire the blooming form of Stepan Arkadyevitch, inhaling the smell of coffee and fresh croissants, we may experience something of that same nostalgia which Tolstoy plainly felt for the social world, viewed not as in *War and Peace* as brutal and depraved but rather as if looking back on childhood—to a world where people were still, as he, Tolstoy, had once been, content to be thus childishly occupied, absorbed, their trivial lives unshadowed by thoughts of death. Some clue to the reason why Tolstoy chose to write, to identify with *Anna,* is provided by the chapter describing Levin's visit to the club—where people leave their troubles behind with their hats in the hall, where everyone is accepted and relaxed. We smell the leather chairs and feel the relief of it all, of this milieu where no women are admitted, where time and money are gambled away, where we see—can it really be true?—the same old faces behind the newspapers.

'Vengeance is mine. I will repay' is the motto of the book. Unlike its predecessor *War and Peace, Anna Karenina* is a fully adult work. Its themes are those of sexual love and death, and, too, that actions have consequences which we can no longer, as when young, lightly leave behind. Later our acts become our lives. We are to blame but we are not to blame. It is this new restraint, a new complexity, that sets the second book above the first.

—Elizabeth Gunn, *A Daring Coiffeur: Reflections on* War and Peace *and* Anna Karenina (London: Chatto and Windus, 1971): pp. 93–95.

# Elisabeth Stenbock-Fermor on Tolstoi's View of Family

[Tolstoi believed the sanctity of family and peasant-based agriculture were the heart and salvation of Russian culture. Stenbock-Fermor discusses the link between these ideas.]

⟨. . .⟩ So Tolstoj considered the family idea as being on the same level of importance as the national idea in *War and Peace,* where every character was somehow connected with the events leading to national victory and liberation from foreign invasion; and the characters are made attractive insofar as they contribute to this victory or sympathize with the common effort. ⟨. . .⟩

To Tolstoj, at that period of his life, marriage was not just the culmination of sexual, spiritual and romantic attraction, though they all were necessary for a man of a certain educational level; neither was its only aim the creation of a couple, with or without children, united by love and understanding—it was the formation of a social unit which could, by its very existence, be a moral and material influence in the country's historical development. ⟨. . .⟩

The good life could only be life connected with agriculture, and this was feasible only if there was a family to help with household chores and work in the fields. Marrying was the right thing to do in order to carry out one's sacred duty, to make the earth productive so that mankind could live contentedly, but not in idleness and luxury. ⟨. . .⟩

⟨F⟩or Tolstoj the monogamous family was not the product of economic interests, centered at first on agriculture for livelihood, becoming later a means to social and economic power, and finally forming tribes, city-states or nations. In Tolstoj's philosophy, reasoning worked the other way around: the family was the origin of physically normal and socially moral life; it was not the product of economic conditions. It was the procreative and productive unit which is the basis for the continuation of life, as ordained by natural law, for all the vegetable and animal species. Man could lift the family principle higher through his human capacity for spiritualizing his aims and loving the members of his family (not only sexual love is involved)—a capacity which belongs to man alone.

Tilling the earth, harvesting, felling trees, making hay, and breeding cattle were sacred occupations, because they produced the necessities for human existence, the continuity of life, while keeping man close to nature. ⟨. . .⟩ Healthy life and physical exertion kept relationships between the sexes in their natural place, with the sole aim of procreation, instead of exasperating sexual appetite and attributing to it an exaggerated importance to human health which, consequently, imposed the humiliation of prostitution, a necessity in the cities where—owing to leisure, overeating and general self-indulgence—sexual desire becomes an aim in itself.

—Elisabeth Stenbock-Fermor, *The Architecture of Anna Karenina: A History of Its Writing, Structure, and Message.* (Belgium: The Peter de Ridder Press, 1975): pp. 77–89.

## E. B. GREENWOOD ON TRAGIC ASPECTS

[The epitaph about revenge suggests to some readers that Tolstoy condemns Anna. In this extract, Greenwood observes that Anna's fate has a tragic inevitability that Tolstoy saw and thus her tragedy is not punishment.]

There is no doubt, however, that the idea 'judge not' is *one* of the main themes of the book. Weitz misses the point that there is a kind of moral paradox here akin to Sir Karl Popper's paradox of tolerance. The hypocritical, frigid and vacuous society that condemns Anna is itself open to condemnation precisely for the reason that it judges. Moreover Anna herself judges too. Her last wish is the moralistic wish to punish Vronsky. No, not quite her last wish, for even as she throws herself under the train she is horrified and prays for forgiveness. That is why Strakhov is not quite right in saying that Tolstoy pursues her pitilessly to the very end.

The tragic situation is a situation from which there is no escape except by the death of the protagonist, whereas it is the essence of comedy that there is always a way out. This point is dramatized in the following discussion between Anna and Oblonsky:

'No, Stiva,' said she, 'I am lost, quite lost! And even worse than lost. I am not lost yet; I cannot say "all is finished": on the contrary, I feel that all is not yet finished. I am like a tightly-strung cord which must snap. But all is not yet finished . . . and it will end in some dreadful manner.'

'Oh no! One can loosen the string gently. There is no situation from which there is no escape.'

'I have been thinking and thinking. Only one. . . .'

Again he understood from her frightened face that she considered death to be the only escape, and did not let her finish.

This dialogue comes about half-way through the novel shortly after Anna has recovered from her illness in giving birth to Vronsky's child. But what about the 'dreadful manner' in which it does end? It is interesting to contrast Tolstoy's portrayal of Anna's death with Flaubert's portrayal of Madame Bovary's. Flaubert throws all the emphasis on the sensuous aspects of Emma, on 'the soles of the feet, that once had run so swiftly to the assuaging of her desires, and now would walk no more.' He savours Emma's sensuous disintegration as he had once savoured her sensuous ecstasies. The touch of the voluptuary is inescapable. But Tolstoy allows Anna a clear *moral* consciousness of her situation and dilemmas right to the end. Her interior monologues on the way to her suicide contain one of the most potent negative visions in the whole of literature: 'Are we not all flung into the world only to hate each other, and therefore to torment ourselves and others?' She wishes to punish Vronsky, as we have seen, until her last 'God forgive me everything!' as the railway truck strikes her. Her original dilemma had been painful, to yield to Vronsky or to continue to be stifled by Karenin. She had committed herself to Vronsky. But then she had found herself demanding a full commitment from him and placing both in a situation from which there was no way out except by her death. We do not feel that Tolstoy indulged her and then got satisfaction out of punishing her. Her fate has a contingency and yet a pattern that bears the marks not of the author's vindictiveness, but of the poetic inevitability we associate with tragedy. Even with her descent into hysteria and morphine addiction Anna is never denied the protection of that aura of dignity with which tragedy always invests its protagonists.

But Tolstoy's comprehensive vision is a vision of the whole truth, and the whole truth is wider than the artistically shaped contingencies of poetic inevitability, encompassing contingency in the raw so to speak. It includes a world in which the real most emphatically is not the rational, a world in which women suffer from pregnancy-sickness and shattered heroes from toothache, and in which a man's whole happiness and everything that makes life meaningful to him may be subject to something as chancy and as artistically non-tragic as a stroke of lightning—the world, in short, of us all. And yet we, like Levin, have the power to invest this meaningless world of chance with the meaning of goodness; for that is its challenge, and our perhaps unique privilege.

—E. B. Greenwood, *Tolstoy: The Comprehensive Vision* (New York: St. Martin's Press, 1975): pp. 117–118.

## Edward Wasiolek on Why Anna Kills Herself

[To the question of Anna's suicide Edward Wasiolek responds by illuminating Tolstoy's dark view of human sexuality. Edward Wasiolek is professor of English and Slavic languages and literature at the University of Chicago. He translated the diaries Dostoevsky kept while writing his famous novels.}

Why does Anna kill herself? The question asks why Anna degenerated from the life-loving, generous and humane person we first meet to the tormented, punishing, strife-ridden and strife-giving person she becomes at the end. One will want to exonerate Anna—to blame society, her husband, Vronsky, and surely to blame the conditions of her love. Good reasons can be found to exonerate her; Tolstoy gives us many. But although he loves Anna and weeps for her, Tolstoy is convinced that she is wrong and that the love she bears for Vronsky is wrong. To show that she is wrong he gives us a picture of the right kind of love in Kitty's and Levin's love. The contrast between those two loves embraces the structure of the novel. Tolstoy has worked out the contrast in a deliberate way. While Anna is falling in love with Vronsky, Levin is being rejected by Kitty. When Kitty and Levin are falling in love, Anna is on her deathbed, attempting to reconcile herself to Karenin, struggling to give up Vronsky. As Anna and Vronsky leave Russia to begin their restless and aimless travels, Kitty and Levin are married. When Anna and Vronsky return to Moscow to make one desperate attempt to get a divorce and resolve their situation, Kitty is having a baby, finding new bonds of love and companionship with Levin. When Anna kills herself, Levin finds the secret of life in the words of an ignorant peasant. By and large the novel describes the deterioration of Anna's and Vronsky's love and the growth toward maturity of Kitty's and Levin's love. ⟨. . .⟩

To account for the difference between Kitty's and Levin's "right" love, and Anna's and Vronsky's "wrong" love, one may say that the former is "natural" and the latter is "unnatural." But it is not so easy to say why one is natural and the other is unnatural. The good marriage for Tolstoy is free of the vanities of social life, fixed in mutual obligation of practical work, characterized by devotion of the partners to each other; most of all it is based on the birth and rearing of children. Levin's and Kitty's union fulfills, or at least comes to fulfill, all of these conditions. But in large measure so does the union of Vronsky and Anna. ⟨. . .⟩

It is the nature of physical passion that works for the destruction of Anna's and Vronsky's love, brings them to hatred of each other, brings Anna to hatred of herself, makes their relationship more and more spectral, breaks down the communication between them, brings them into a situation where they cannot speak frankly to each other, makes them avoid certain subjects, and forces them to surround themselves with other people so as to make each other's presence tolerable. Kitty's and Levin's relationship, on the other hand, is free of passion: they argue, work together; they feel close and at moments drift apart; they love each other and the love grows and prospers, but there is no indication on the part of either that the body of each is in some way the basis of their closeness. Kitty's and Levin's union is uncontaminated by sex. ⟨. . .⟩ The work of each is serious in a way that the activities of Anna and Vronsky are not. ⟨. . .⟩

Tolstoy sees sex as a massive intrusion on a person's being and a ruthless obliteration of the sanctity of personhood. Both Anna and Vronsky feel coerced and manipulated by the other. The stronger Anna loves, the more she coerces and the more she alienates. The corrupting power of sex seems to be an extreme example of what Tolstoy has always been against: the attempt of the individual to make the world one's own and the consequent impoverishing and desiccating effect that such coercion has on the world about one.

—Edward Wasiolek, *Critical Essays on Tolstoy,* ed. Edward Wasiolek (Boston: G. K. Hall & Co., 1986) pp. 150–151, 153–154.

## Malcolm Jones on Problems of Communication

[Jones discusses defects of communication resulting from deception as central to Anna's tragedy. He is senior lecturer in Russian at the University of Nottingham.]

⟨T⟩here is a two-fold failure to communicate at the very heart of the Anna–Vronsky relationship, and the problem is never resolved. Anna cannot share her deepest and most imperious feelings with her lover, and she suppresses them and banishes them from her own consciousness. Of course, there is always the possibility that Anna may overcome these emotional difficulties, and that possibility carries the fiction on for six more books, but it can be seen in retrospect that she never regains her emotional security, except superficially by closing her eyes to some crucial aspect of her situation, an attitude which she cannot forever sustain and which becomes a source of frustration and despair to Vronsky. ⟨...⟩

There is another subject on which Anna cannot communicate with Vronsky, and this comes close to the heart of their tragedy. It is her son, Seriozha. Even before the question of deserting him arises, Seriozha has becomes a standing reproach to them both. ⟨...⟩

There are times when Anna closes her eyes to Seriozha too. But he represents her last emotional prop as well as having been the beneficiary of her love during her marriage. ⟨...⟩

Karenin too resolves to cut off communication with his wife on intimate matters and, like Anna, he also stops thinking about his marital problems. He does not want to think about them and actually succeeds in not doing so. Neither husband nor wife will permit themselves to think of the other's real emotional state, and the physical revulsion which Anna has experienced in her reactions to Karenin is now extended to the spiritual realm as well. She sees him now not as a remarkable man, but as a hypocrite who cares only about pretence and propriety and has no feelings. It is, after all, but a short step from a refusal to discern another's feelings to a denial that he has any. ⟨. . .⟩

Looks and glances, tones of voice, become the currency of interchange and an inadequate substitute for mutual confidence. They do not now lead in to the heart: they forbid entry, and as Karenin had once reacted by murmuring to himself 'so much the worse for her', so now Vronsky has recourse to the same reaction. What is more, as Anna's fevered imagination runs ahead of reality she takes Vronsky's cool looks to heart, seeing in them evidence of a cooling passion and perhaps something much worse. It is this something worse, for which she has not a shred of evidence, which makes her panic. The more she is convinced that he is tiring of her, the more counterproductive her attempts to hang on to him become. ⟨. . .⟩

⟨I⟩n the end Levin has a number of great advantages over Anna: he looks life full in the face and shuts out nothing of consequence from his range of vision; and he has the emotional security and social acceptability of a respectable married life to sustain him. ⟨. . .⟩ The details may remain his secret, but the underlying emotions are shared. This is the crux of the matter: Levin wants to share his deepest emotions with his wife; he is bitterly unhappy when he fails, and in the end he succeeds, not least because he trusts in the promptings of his conscience. If all this seems too neat, it must be remembered that Levin's problems are immense and his path is far from easy. The reader may doubt, moreover, whether at the close of the novel they are truly at an end. Insofar as there is a moral to this story, it does, of course, have its controversial aspects, but it is difficult to fault Tolstoy's psychology.

—Malcolm Jones, *New Essays on Tolstoy,* ed. Malcom Jones (Cambridge: Cambridge University Press,1978): pp. 101–103, 104–105, 107.

## JOAN DELANEY GROSSMAN ON COMMUNICATION AS A FEATURE OF CHARACTER

[In her study of language in *Anna Karenina,* Grossman observes that difficulty in communication signals a defect of character. Grossman is chair of Slavic languages and literature at the University of California at Berkeley.]

These several scenes, whatever else their purpose, clearly focus attention on the function of dialogue in character dynamics and their depiction. This was hardly a new concern for a novelist, and mid-nineteenth-century realism especially demanded a keen ear for language and for social intonation. Tolstoy's own art in this regard had reached a high degree of perfection. However, he here seems particularly struck by what happens when discourse conventions break down.

The scenes in Betsy's drawing room are necessary counterweights to the passages where Anna and Vronsky face each other alone. In the first sequence, the contrast is only sketched. Even à deux they do not depart decisively from their initial roles as society seducer and reluctant quarry. But in the second sequence, where all is focused on Anna's situation, contrasting elements are sharpened. The lesson of Betsy's drawing room is that skillful handling of a situation on the level of social discourse and behavior by that very fact prevents its becoming socially troublesome. No other level of concern is recognized. But when Anna meets Vronsky in the Vrede garden, Betsy's lessons are of no help. There is no counterpoint, either of clever conversation or of literary scenario. Tolstoy now lets his characters fend for themselves. And when most needed, their resources in the matter of communication are pitifully thin. They fall back, in Vronsky's case, on inbred social patterns—how a gentleman responds to an outraged husband's challenge—and in Anna's on fantasy from high romance: "Give up everything and fly with me!" Each hears only his or her own thoughts, and the rustle of emotions prevents them from hearing even these clearly. Each is inarticulate in his or her own way. Their failure to establish a coherent dialogue reflects the inability to address each other's real concerns and expectations and, at the same time, to listen deeply to themselves. Here revealed, then, are the basic contradictions in character and conditioning that will shape their behavior from now to the catastrophe.

—Joan Delayney Grossman, *In the Shade of the Giant: Essays on Tolstoy,* ed. Hugh McLean (Berkeley: University of California Press, 1989): pp. 127–128.

## Natasha Sankovitch on Forgiveness

[Tolstoy's epigraph about the Lord's vengeance stands in judgment of Tolstoy's characters which Sankovitch argues is balanced by themes of forgiveness.]

In *Anna Karenina* Tolstoy explores the concept of understanding not just as a cognitive and intellectual faculty, but as an emotional, psychological, and moral force. Forgiveness, a special kind of understanding between two people because of the demands it makes on both of them, becomes a theme in this novel in which relations between man and woman are turbulent and uncertain even when love is present. ⟨. . .⟩

The numerous repetitions of "forgiveness" in various contexts, as the expression of individual characters' capacity for moving outward beyond the self to extend sympathy, understanding, and love to others, stand in opposition to the novel's terse epigraph: "Vengeance is mine; I shall repay." For Orthodox believers, the ultimate power for both vengeance and forgiveness resides in God. Tolstoy himself seems to have accepted this truism, but he also knew that behind human acts of vengeance and forgiveness stands a vast array of individual moral and psychological attitudes and motives. In *Anna Karenina* vengeance remains for the most part an unstated, yet subtly present, theme. As Anna's fate demonstrates, vengeance can never be the starting point for understanding or love. At least in part, Anna's suicide is an act of vengeance, an act intended to punish Vronsky; with death, however, the possibility for any further communication ends. Forgiveness, on the other hand, sincerely felt and honestly expressed, begins with an act of understanding. The explicit repetitions of "forgiveness" testify to the positive potentials it contains even if these potentials are only rarely or briefly attained.

With the themes of forgiveness and "what can you do?" Tolstoy explores what the quality of characters' relations with other characters suggests about them as individuals. At times, acts of forgiveness and utterances of "what can you do?" become a form of self-deception, a way of structuring one's relation to another in terms of an established moral, religious, or social attitude, that relieves one of having to find one's own attitude. The repetition of these expressions not only establishes them as paradigms for viewing a conflict, but undermines their stability as such by illustrating various individual appropriations of the paradigmatic concept.

Moral absolutes and traditional values come under scrutiny in *Anna Karenina* as characters struggle to strike a balance in their lives between social and familial expectations and responsibilities, and personal happiness and fulfillment, between altruism and egoism. The task for Tolstoy's characters is to weave together a particular version of how to live (a morality, a set of rules, a narrative) both personal and tied to external (social, military, religious, novelistic) tradition. In a world where morality is not a matter of rules, cannot be generalized, a moral sense is developed by learning to make fine distinctions among apparently similar cases. Repetition reminds us of these similarities so we can attend to differences as part of our moral education. As with morality, so with authenticity, a life lived truly is a matter of sensitively appropriate responses to particular situations.

—Natasha Sankovitch, *Creating and Recovering Experience: Repetition in Tolstoy* (Stanford: Stanford University Press, 1998): pp. 156, 162–163.

## JAMES WOOD ON THE NEW TRANSLATION

[In this review from *The New Yorker* James Wood praises the most recent translation of *Anna Karenina* for its fresh rendering of Tolstoy's masterful use of realistic detail.]

Everyone who reads Tolstoy feels that it is an experience different in kind, not just degree, from reading the other great novelists. But how, and why? ⟨. . .⟩ The transparency of Tolstoy's art—realism as a kind of neutral substrate, like air—makes it very difficult to account for, and more often than not one blusters in tautologies. Why are his characters so real? ⟨. . .⟩ Even Tolstoy himself was forced into paradox when defending his work. ⟨. . .⟩ he argued that his writings were not collections of ideas that could be abstracted from the text but a network: "This network itself is not made up of ideas (or so I think), but of something else, and it is absolutely impossible to express the substance of this network directly in words: it can be done only indirectly, by using words to describe characters, acts, situations."

This letter is quoted by Richard Pevear in his fine introduction to the new translation that he and Larissa Volokhonsky have produced of "Anna Karenina ⟨. . .⟩. Great translations age, while great novels merely mature, and it would be valuable to have even an ordinary contemporary English version of Tolstoy's book. But Pevear and Volokhonsky are at once scrupulous translators and vivid stylists of English, and their superb rendering allows us, as perhaps never before, to grasp the palpability of Tolstoy's "characters, acts, situations."

The novel's opening provides an example of Tolstoy's easy fullness, and of this translation's happy loyalty to it. Stiva Oblonsky—vigorous and wellborn, simple, handsome, "cheerful and content," the possessor of a habitually kind smile—has been having an affair with the former governess of his children. Unfortunately, his wife Dolly, has found out, and Stiva miserably recalls the recent evening when, returning from the theatre and "holding a huge pear for his wife" (we are two pages into the novel, and already Tolstoy's succulence of detail is bearing fruit), he found her not in the drawing room but in their bedroom, holding an incriminating letter.

But Stiva is incapable of depression. Like many of Tolstoy's men, he has a self-sufficiency that verges on egoism. Like Shakespeare's, Tolstoy's characters feel real to us in part because they feel so real to themselves, take their own universes for granted. What can Stiva do about his wife's unhappiness? Life tells him to go on living, in obliviousness, and that is all. In effect, he forgets about it. He takes what is clearly a customary pleasure in the rituals of waking and dressing. ⟨. . .⟩ we see him "drawing a goodly amount of air into the broad box of his chest," going to the window "with the customary brisk step of his splayed feet, which so easily carried his full body." A barber arrives, and with his "glossy, plump little hand" sets about "clearing a pink path between his long, curly side-whiskers." 〈. . .〉

Always, in Pevear and Volokhonsky's version, we feel the physicality of Tolstoy's details. Rosemary Edmonds, who translated the novel for the Penguin edition in 1954, is more muted. In her English, we see Stiva merely "drawing a deep breath into his powerful lungs," where Pevear and Volokhonsky have "the broad box of his chest"; Stiva's "splayed feet," a detail that marvellously registers the man's heavy displacement, is in Edmonds "his usual spirited step, carrying his vigorous body lightly." The barber's "pink path" is, in Edmonds, a duller "rosy parting."

—James Woods, *The New Yorker* (February 5, 2001): pp. 82, 87. Reprinted by permission.

# Works by Leo Tolstoy

*Childhood.* 1852.

*Adolescence.* 1854.

*Sevastopol Sketches.* 1855–56.

*Youth.* 1857.

*The Cossacks.* 1863.

*War and Peace.* 1873.

*A New Primer.* 1875.

*A Russian Reader.* 1875.

*Anna Karenina.* 1877.

*A Confession.* 1882.

*The Death of Ivan Ilyich.* 1886.

*The Kreutzer Sonata.* 1890.

*What Is Art?* 1897.

*The Resurrection.* 1899.

*Hadji Murat.* 1904.

# Works About
# Leo Tolstoy

Benson, Ruth Crego. *Women in Tolstoy: The Ideal and the Erotic.* Chicago: University of Chicago Press, 1973.

Blackmur, R. P. *Eleven Essays on Nineteenth Century Novel.* New York: Harcourt, Brace and World, 1964.

Christian, R. F. *Tolstoy's* War and Peace: *A Study.* Oxford: Clarendon Press, 1962.

Farrell, James T. *Literature and Morality.* New York: The Vanguard Press, Inc., 1945.

Gifford, Henry. *Tolstoy.* Oxford: Oxford University Press, 1982.

Goscilo, Helena and Petre Petrov, eds. Anna Karenina *on Page and Screen.* Pittsburgh, Pennsylvania: University of Pittsburgh, 2001.

Greenwood, E. B. *Tolstoy: The Comprehensive Vision.* New York: St. Martin's Press, 1975.

Gunn, Elizabeth. *A Daring Coiffeur: Reflections on* War and Peace *and* Anna Karenina. London: Chatto and Windus, 1971.

Jones, Malcolm, ed. *New Essays on Tolstoy.* Cambridge: Cambridge University Press, 1978.

Leon, Derrick. *Tolstoy: His Life and Work.* London: Routledge, 1944.

Lubbock, Percy. *The Craft of Fiction.* New York: Viking, 1964.

Matlaw, Ralph E. ed. *Tolstoy: A Collection of Critical Essays.* Englewood Cliffs, New Jersey: Prentice Hall, Inc., 1967.

McLean, Hugh, ed. *In the Shade of the Giant: Essays on Tolstoy.* Berkeley: University of California Press, 1989.

Morson, Gary Saul. *Hidden in Plain View: Narrative and Creative Potentials in* War and Peace. Stanford: Stanford University Press, 1987.

Poggioli, Renato. *The Spirit of the Letter.* Cambridge: Harvard University Press, 1965.

Price, Martin. *Forms of Life: Character and Moral Imagination in the Novel.* New Haven: Yale University Press, 1983.

Rancour-Laferriere, Daniel. *Tolstoy's Pierre Bezukhov: A Psychoanalytic Study.* London: Bristol Classical Press, 1993.

Silbajoris, R. War and Peace: *Tolstoy's Mirror of the World.* New York: Twayne Publishers, 1995.

Simmons, Ernest J. *Introduction to Tolstoy's Writings.* Chicago: University of Chicago Press, 1968.

Stenbock-Fermor, Elizabeth. *The Architecture of* Anna Karenina*: A History of Its Writing, Structure, and Message.* Belgium: The Peter De Ridder Press, 1975.

Thorlby, Anthony. *Leo Tolstoy,* Anna Karenina. Cambridge, Cambridge University Press, 1987.

Trilling, Lionel. *The Opposing Self.* New York: Viking Press, 1959.

Wasiolek, Edward. *Tolstoy's Major Fiction.* Chicago, University of Chicago Press, 1978.

————— , ed. *Critical Essays on Tolstoy.* Boston: G. K. Hall and Co., 1986.

Wood, James. "At Home in the World." *The New Yorker.* February 5, 2001.

# Index of
# Themes and Ideas

in, 21, 22, 24, 27; Kuragin family in, 20, 21, 23–24, 43, 45; Kutuzov in, 19, 21, 22, 24; and Lenin's criticism of anti-revolutionary attitudes, 30–32; and moral character, 41–42; and moral originality, 37–38; Nikolai in, 23, 43, 44, 45; Anna Pavlovna in, 18, 24, 37, 41, 42; and peace, 17, 18–19, 20; plot summary of, 17–22; and realism, 28–30, 51–52, 54–56, 67; and repetition, 18, 54–56; Rostov family in, 18, 19, 22, 23; Anatole Kuragin in, 24, 43; Hyppolite Kuragin in, 24; Julie Kuragin in, 24; Natalya Rostova in, 23; Natasha Rostova in, 19, 20, 21, 22, 23, 27, 28, 29, 33, 43, 44, 45; Nikolay Rostov in, 19, 20, 21, 22, 23, 29; Old Count Rostov in, 23; Petya Rostov in, 21, 23, 29; Prince Vassily Kuragin in, 19, 24, 41, 42; Princess Helene Kuragina in, 19, 20, 21, 24, 43; Vera Rostova in, 23; Countess Rostova in, 23; and Shakespeare, 10–11; Sonia in, 19, 23; Tolstoy's purpose for writing, 17; Turgenev's irritation and satisfaction with, 25–26; and understanding of life, 18, 20, 21–22, 34–35; as "unrest of life itself," 26–28; and vitalistic simplification, 35–37; and war, 17, 18, 19–21, 22; and "Why Live?", 20, 34–35